Introduct

Lying within Snowdonia National Park
of Betws-y-Coed, is a little known area oı aɯ˙˙
enclosed upland pasture, open hills, forest and moorland. Wɪuɪɪɪ ˙
fascinating landscape can be found two historic Welsh speaking villages.

Penmachno stands in the beautiful secluded fertile Machno valley, on an
important drovers' route and near Roman roads. St Tudclud's church built
in 1859 on the site of two earlier churches, contains several inscribed late
5thC/mid 6thC stones, providing evidence of early Christianity in the area.
This traditional farming community grew during the 19thC and contained
over 1,700 people by 1871, boosted by work at a nearby woollen mill and
slate quarrying at Cwm Penmachno, an important quarry village. Ysbyty
Ifan ('hospice of John'), lying a few miles to the east, stands at an important
crossing point of the Conwy river on a network of ancient routes to Anglesey,
Bardsey Island, Mid-Wales, Chester and London, used by drovers, travellers
and pilgrims. Around 1190 the Hospitaler Knights of St John of Jerusalem
built a church and hospice here, which for many years provided shelter and
refreshment for those who passed by. The village was also famous for its
animal fairs, which attracted cattle dealers from far and wide.

Much of the area, encompassing the Machno, Eidda and Upper Conwy
valleys, is part of the Ysbyty estate, once owned by Lord Penrhyn, and since
1951 managed by the National Trust. It is one of the Trust's largest agricultural
estates, featuring over 50 tenant farms. It is a delightful area to explore on
foot, with a good Rights of Way network, which has recently been upgraded.

The 24 walks in this book visit places of interest, including Tŷ Mawr, old
slate quarries, upland reservoirs, and waterfalls. They feature old drovers'
routes, a stunning upland quarry tramway, and breathtaking views. They
range from easy valley walks to more demanding hill and moorland treks.

The routes follow public rights of way, forestry tracks or cross Open
Access land, and are within the capability of most people. Many individual
routes contain shorter walk options and can easily be linked with others
to provide longer day walks, if required. Walking boots are recommended,
along with appropriate clothing to protect against the elements. Be properly
prepared and equipped, especially on the higher routes. Please remember that
path conditions can vary according to season and weather.

Each walk has a detailed map and description which enables the route
to be followed without difficulty. Bear in mind though that changes in detail
can occur at any time. The location of each walk is shown on the back cover
and a summary of their key features is also given. This includes an estimated
walking time, but allow more time to enjoy the scenery.

Please observe The Country Code. Enjoy your walking!

CWM GLASGWM

DESCRIPTION A 5¾ mile walk (**A**), exploring the attractive part wooded Glasgwm valley. The route follows a minor road up into the valley, then crosses fields via Plas Glasgwm to Coed Pen-y-bryn. It then follows a forestry track up alongside the delightful infant Glasgwm river into the head of the valley, reaching a height of 1181 feet/360 metres, before returning across more open slopes offering extensive views, then descending through mixed woodland to join the valley road. It then continues through further forest before descending to Penmachno. Allow about 3½ hours. An alternative lower level 4½ mile walk (**B**) is included. The valley road offers other shorter walk options.

START The Eagles, Penmachno [SH 790506].

I From The Eagles go along the minor road signposted to Ty Mawr, soon crossing the Afon Glasgwm. Continue along the road past Bron-y-Graig, after which it rises then continues beneath the forest – *with a good view along the part-forested Glasgwm valley and across to the bare top of Moel-Pen-y-bryn standing proud above the trees.* When the road splits take the left fork. Almost immediately take a signposted path through a gate on the left. Angle away from the boundary down across the field to go through a wide gap in the hedge ahead. Go across the next large field just below cables, then follow a line of mature trees to go through a gate in the corner. Go along the left-hand side of the tree boundary then angle down to a stile in the fence on your left just before a stone barn. Pass round the left-hand side of the barn to a gate, then cross a stream just ahead where it joins the Afon Glasgwm. Continue along the farm track, then just before it enters a field turn RIGHT up alongside a stream to a gate below Plas Glasgwm. Go up a faint green track then cross the farmyard and continue between buildings to gates. Pass to the right of the small building just ahead and go along the edge of the access track to go through a gate ahead above a stream.

2 Go down the stony track to cross a bridge over the Afon Glasgwm. Continue along the green track to pass above a corrugated barn, through a gate and on to pass in front of a cottage. After a stream and a gate keep ahead through a reedy field to a stile into the forest. A path rises steadily through the mature pines to a stony forestry track. Follow it RIGHT – *soon with a view into the valley* – to a track junction. (For **Walk B** turn right down the track to a gate and cross a bridge over the river to a cottage. Follow its rough access road along Cwm Glasgwm. After a gate continue along the narrow road beneath woodland, passing above a cottage and enjoying views of the river in the valley below. Shortly the road passes the access track leading down to hidden Plas Glasgwm, rises past Plas Newydd then levels out and is joined by a forestry track – Walk A – angling in on the left. Resume instructions in paragraph **4**.)

3 For **Walk A** continue up the track above the river, past side tracks leading to near-by dwellings. At a track junction keep ahead up the narrow track, soon joined by a bike trail. The track continues to rise alongside the infant river, past a series of small cascades, through an increasingly open section of forest. At a crossroad of tracks, with a view of the bare ridge of Y Ro Wen ahead, turn RIGHT on the waymarked red bike trail, passing over the river. The track contours across the forested slope – *with good views down into the wooded valley* – then gently descends, with the bike trail running beneath it – *enjoying panoramic views.* When the track rises half-left keep ahead down an old track and through the forest, twice intercepting with the bike trail. It then begins a long gradual descent through the forest then deciduous woodland, being crossed by the bike trail, to eventually join a minor road. Keep ahead.

4 About 100 yards further just before the road crosses a narrow wooded gorge, take a path angling off on the left. It crosses a stream then bends away from the road and rises steadily through the

The head of Cwm Glasgwm

trees to join a minor road. Turn RIGHT then almost immediately LEFT up a forestry track. At a crossroad of tracks turn RIGHT down beneath a cottage (Pen Top) and follow the track through the mixed woodland. After just over ½ mile, after passing a rough track

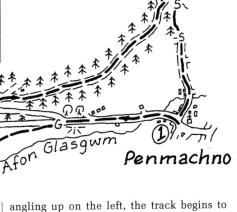

angling up on the left, the track begins to descend and crosses a major stream at an area of cleared forest. About 10 yards beyond turn RIGHT down a wide meandering path to cross a stile and the stream beyond. Follow the enclosed path down to the forest corner, then descend the short steep slope to a ladder-stile. Go down the access track and on past Ty'n-y ddol, then follow its access lane over the river and on into Penmachno.

WALK 2

MOEL PEN-Y-BRYN

DESCRIPTION A meandering 5 mile walk, featuring a distinctive part forested hill overlooking Penmachno, and ever changing views. The route follows forestry tracks up through Coed Pen-y-bryn to a point allowing access for a short climb onto the wide tussocky, heather, reedy summit of Moel Pen-y-bryn (1404 feet/428 metres) offering extensive all-round views. It then returns by forestry tracks. Allow about 3 ½ hours. Note that the views change according to tree growth and felling.

START Car park, Coed Pen-y-bryn [SH 786497].

DIRECTIONS From Penmachno follow the road south towards Cwm Penmachno. After ½ mile you reach the wide entrance to Coed Pen-y-bryn. The car park lies a little way up the stony forestry track and is the start of mountain bike trails maintained by the local community.

1 Continue up the forestry track to a junction at a good viewpoint. Here do a sharp U-turn on the signposted red mountain bike trail. Follow the track up the hillside – *enjoying good views into the Machno valley and to the Foel Boeth ridge* – to a bend – *offering new views down to Penmachno and east along the valley*. Continue up the track past where the bike trail angles into the trees, then down to a track junction.

2 Follow the track ahead, rising steadily through the mature forest, briefly joined by the bike trail. At a large track junction in an open area of forest do a sharp U-turn LEFT and follow the level track back north east. After a view down into Cwm Glasgwm by inclined exposed rock slabs, the track begins to descend, shortly passing another viewpoint east along the Machno valley towards distant Mynydd Hiraethog. The track then bends southwards and rises steadily. At the end of conifers on your right you reach the open upper slopes of Moel Pen-y-bryn.

3 Cross a stile in the fence up on your right and follow the adjoining wall up through bracken to join a clear cross path a few yards above. Follow it RIGHT through bracken, soon climbing steadily beside the forest perimeter across bracken, tussocky and heather terrain. Shortly the path levels out and crosses a reedy area to a good viewpoint looking east along the Machno valley, where the ground begins to descend. Here leave the path and turn LEFT up the tussocky slope and go across the northern end of Moel Pen-y-bryn to its side overlooking the forested Cwm Glasgwm – *enjoying panoramic views*. Now head across the hill's flat top to its southern end – *offering good views to Cwm Penmachno and its old slate quarry*. Work you way down the tussocky, heather and reedy slope back to the stile, using the distant wall as your guide. Continue with the track past Moel Pen-y-bryn's open slopes, then through the forest, later heading towards the ridge of Y Ro Wen to reach a track T-junction. Turn LEFT.

4 At a crossing of tracks, turn LEFT and follow the track down through the forest, shortly being joined by the bike trail. The track contours across the wooded slope past viewpoints, later descending to join your outward route.

WALK 3

COED PEN-Y-BRYN

DESCRIPTION A 4¼ mile undulating walk exploring the Forestry Commission woodland of Coed Pen-y-bryn near Penmachno. The route follows forestry tracks and paths, enjoying good views into both the Glasgwm and Machno valleys. Allow about 3 hours.

START Car park, Coed Pen-y-bryn [SH 786497].

1 Follow instructions in paragraph **1** of Walk 2.

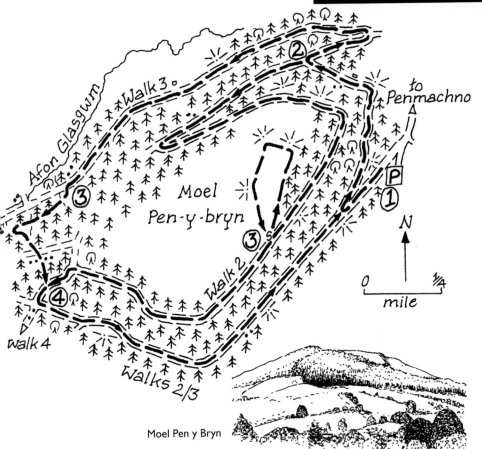

Moel Pen y Bryn

2 Here turn sharp RIGHT down the stony forestry track. At a track junction – *with a view to Penmachno and along the lower Machno valley* – the main track does a sharp U-turn and is soon enclosed by trees. It continues through the mixed woodland, later rising alongside telegraph poles then crossing an area of cleared forest – *with a view down into the wooded Glasgwm valley* – and passing above a small stone ruin. After becoming enclosed by trees once more the track passes an old green track angling up on the left. Shortly the track begins to descend through am area of mature trees and you are joined by a waymarked path coming in from the right.

3 A few yards beyond take another way-marked path on the left up through the trees. After crossing a stream the path continues through the dense forest, then crosses another stream. At a waymark post just before a fence and house in a small clearing, turn LEFT to the fence corner. A waymark in a tree ahead marks a path leading LEFT up through conifers, soon angling LEFT across a small clearing and up through more conifers to a forestry track. Take the nearby way-marked path up through trees, over a mountain bike trail and on up to another stony forestry track. Follow it RIGHT to a crossing of tracks.

4 Follow instructions in paragraph **4** of Walk 2.

5

UPPER MACHNO VALLEY

DESCRIPTION A 5½ mile (**A**) or 5 mile (**B**) walk around the upper Machno valley. The route first follows a forestry track around the lower forest covered slopes of Moel Pen-y-bryn past several good viewpoints, then descends a path through the forest. Walk A continues on paths down to Cwm Penmachno village, then follows the valley road east to pass through Carrog. Walk B heads east then descends to the valley road. Both walks then follow the river along the attractive valley. Allow about 3½ hours.
START Car park, Coed Pen-y-bryn [SH 786497].
DIRECTIONS See Walk 2.

1 Follow the stony forestry track up to a junction at a good viewpoint, then continue ahead up the track. Follow it for 1¼ miles past viewpoints and a track on the left to reach a crossroad of tracks. Turn LEFT on the signposted red bike trail, shortly descending, then take a waymarked path on the left down through conifers to another stony track. The path continues opposite through the forest gradually descending to another stony track. (For **Walk B** turn left and follow instructions in paragraph **2** of Walk 5 to the road. After crossing the bridge over the river go through an iron gate on the left then follow instructions in paragraph **3**.)

2 For **Walk A** take the waymarked path ahead through mature trees, past an old ruin and down the forest edge to a stile. Follow the path down the middle of the field to a ladder-stile and footbridge over the stream. Go up the slope ahead and bear LEFT down the field edge to a gate at the back of houses to reach the nearby road in Cwm Penmachno. Follow the road LEFT out of the village to the junction at Carrog. Continue east along the valley road. Just before it bends across a bridge over the river, go through an iron gate on the right.

3 Go along the field's right hand edge to a gate by a stream. Keep ahead across the next large field to another gate, then follow a farm track to Pen-y-bedw. Go past outbuildings and the house then down its access track. Just before it crosses a bridge over the river, turn RIGHT on a signposted path. Go along a wide initially reedy old green lane to a gate above the river. Go along the walled track, through another gate at sheep pens, then an adjoining small gate on the left. Turn RIGHT across a small fenced area to a nearby gate and continue across the slope to pass a wall corner with a bridge over the river nearby. Go along the raised edge of the next field, soon joining a nearby farm track to go through a gate ahead. Follow the green track to another gate, then continue along the edge of a reedy stream to cross a large footbridge over the river – *a great place to stop* – and a nearby ladder-stile onto the road. Continue along the road to the entrance to Coed-Pen-y-bryn.

Footbridge over Afon Machno

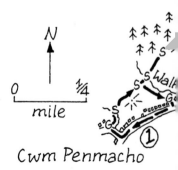

N

0   ¼

mile

Cwm Penmacho

WALK 5

CWM PENMACHNO

DESCRIPTION A 3 mile walk around the upper Machno valley near the former quarrying village of Cwm Penmachno. The route rises on field paths to the forest edge then continues east before descending to the valley road, which it follows back through Carrog to the village.
START Cwm Penmachno [SH 757476].
DIRECTIONS Follow the valley road to Cwm Penmachno to find roadside parking adjoining a gap in houses.

Cwm Penmachno was once a bustling Welsh speaking slate quarry community,with many shops, chapels, a church, pub and a school. See Walk 6 for information on its quarrying history.

I Continue along the road then just past single story terraced cottages turn RIGHT

down the field edge to cross a ladder-stile. Turn LEFT down to cross a nearby footbridge and ladder-stile. Follow the path up the middle of the field to a stile in the top corner, then up the edge of the forest, past a stone ruin and on up to a forestry track. Turn RIGHT.

2 Follow the track to a turning area. Here do a sharp U-turn RIGHT down a waymarked path, soon bending LEFT and continuing along an old rough track through a clearing. At the end of the track turn LEFT up a wide path into the forest. After a few yards it bears RIGHT across two streams, then another (large pipe) at the forest edge. Go up the slope to a hidden stile then across the midslopes of the reedy field to a gate in the fence ahead. Cross the stream beyond and follow a faint

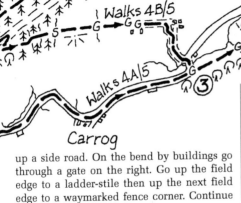

green track along the edge of two fields, through a gate then past a nearby barn to a gate ahead. Pass to the left of the house and go along its access track to a cattle grid. Continue down the track, soon bending RIGHT over another cattle grid past nearby Llechwedd Hafod farm. Follow the stony access track down to the road. Turn RIGHT across the bridge over the river and continue along the road to Carrog. Take the road towards Cwm Penmachno, later passing an impressive chapel and crossing over the river to return to the start

up a side road. On the bend by buildings go through a gate on the right. Go up the field edge to a ladder-stile then up the next field edge to a waymarked fence corner. Continue

WALK 6

RHIW BACH QUARRY

DESCRIPTION A fascinating 6 mile walk (**A**) for experienced hill walkers exploring an upland landscape of hidden slate quarries and reservoirs above Cwm Penmachno, now an Open Access area, enjoying extensive views. The route meanders up through Rhiw Fachno quarry into open country then continues up through impressive Rhiw bach quarry. A delightful tramway then contours at 1607 feet/490 metres across the quarried hillside to Cwy-y-bugail quarry, from where the route can be shortened to a 3¾ mile walk (**B**), and continues past attractive Llyn Bowydd. The next section involves free range walking around part of Llyn Newydd and across pathless tussocky/heather terrain back to Cwy-y-bugail quarry. After crossing rough upland pasture, the route descends alongside a forest to Cwm Penmachno. Allow about 4½ hours. Avoid in poor visibility. An easier alternative 5½ mile walk to fully absorb this unique complex industrial landscape is to follow the good route to instruction **3** then return the same way.
START Quarry entrance, Cwm Penmachno [SH 753472].
DIRECTIONS Follow the road through Cwm Penmachno village to quarry spoil heaps and recycling facilities on the final bend, where there are parking spaces.

In the wild inhospitable hills above the village, men toiled at several remote slate quarries, in all kinds of weather. Quarrying first started at Rhiw bach in the early 19thC and slate was carried by horse down to Cwm Penmachno and taken to Trifriw for loading onto boats. With the opening in 1863 of a high level narrow gauge tramway, enabling slate to be transported via three inclines down to Blaenau Ffestiniog, and on by the Ffestiniog railway to Porthmadog, quarrying grew in scale. Rhiw bach quarry dug deep pits and developed extensive underground workings at 8 different levels. In the 1880s 130 men worked here. Its remoteness led to the creation on site of houses for families,

barracks for men, a shop and schoolroom/ chapel. Concerts and eisteddfodau were held here. The quarry closed in 1951. Blaen-y-cwm quarry, the smallest, closed in 1914. Cwt-y-bugail quarry, which in the 1870s employed 116 men, was the last to close in 1962.

■ From the nearby stile/ gate follow the signposted path along the stony track into the substantial former opencast quarry of Rhiw Fachno. It soon bends left, then right and climbs steadily past tips and an old incline. Continue up the wide stony path, shortly with a stream below, then follow a narrow green path up to a ladder-stile/gate into open country. Follow the stony path above the stream, past the breached dam of a small reservoir – *whose water powered the quarry machinery* – and on to a stile/gate. Follow the wide path through the forest, over a stream and on across open ground towards the extensive Rhiw bach quarry. Keep with the wide green path (a former tramway) above the river, soon with a huge quarry hole to your right. It then rises between spoil heaps up an old incline to a large level working area, with the remains of dressing sheds. Continue to a ladder-stile/gate near the large chimney of a former steam engine house. *This provided power for quarry machinery, and for hauling loaded wagons of slate up the nearby exit incline and others underground.* Pass behind the chimney then walk up the impressive long incline. Continue along the former tramway gradually bending north across the hillside above Blaen-y-cwm quarry.

2 Later the tramway reaches Cwt-y-bugail quarry and splits. (For **Walk B** take its right fork to reach ruined buildings at point 4.) For **Walk A** take the left fork, then a path above the tramway to a ladder-stile. *Ahead are views across Llyn Bowydd to the Moelwyns, Cnicht and Snowdon.* Continue with the path, soon rejoining the tramway, which runs above the southern side of the lake. It then crosses its substantial dam – *with new views to quarries above hidden Blaenau Ffestiniog, a mere 1¼ miles*

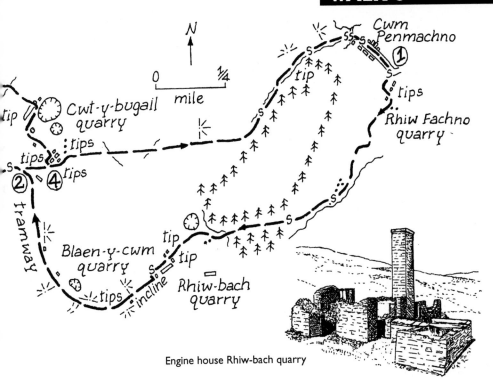

Engine house Rhiw-bach quarry

away. *Soon ahead is the substantial walled dam of hidden Llyn Newydd. Water from both reservoirs is used in Llechwedd quarry to generate hydro electricity. The tramway briefly descends to cross the lake's outflow by a large pipe, then rises to two old concrete pillars.*

3 Here turn RIGHT across reedy ground to a post above the corner of the lake. Now work your way along the lake's heather covered western edge or stony shoreline, then along its northern edge, before continuing eastwards across tussocky/reedy ground. After crossing a stream go up the heather covered higher ground ahead, then aim for the left-hand end of distant spoil heaps at Cwt-y-bugail quarry. Later, work your way LEFT along the edge of a reedy/peaty gully about 100 yards from a fence, then angle RIGHT to cross a wooden section of the fence. Keep ahead to the end of the spoil heap onto an old tramway, with a small stone structure to your left and a huge quarry hole ahead. Descend, then turn RIGHT beneath the spoil heap. At its end keep ahead, passing to the right of a deep shaft [KEEP AWAY] – then between a stone structure and a wall. Bear LEFT to a nearby building. Turn LEFT then RIGHT alongside a short wall and on to two stone supports at the top of an old incline. Descend to ruined buildings below. Turn RIGHT to their end to join the nearby tramway.

4 Follow the tramway past the buildings. As it begins to rise pass close to its right-hand side to join a green path running between waste. Soon turn LEFT to the base of the nearby large tip, then descend beneath it. At the end of the tip on your right work your way eastwards across tussocky terrain towards the left-hand end of the distant forest. Follow the edge of the forest down increasingly steep ground towards Cwm Penmachno, passing a spoil heap and crossing two ladder-stiles, then descend a reedy field to a further ladder-stile. Turn RIGHT over the stream to cross a ladder-stile ahead and another stream. Go past an old barn and on to a ladder-stile/gate Go along the road past terraced houses then a children's playground to the start.

WALK 7
BWLCH Y GROES & TŶ MAWR

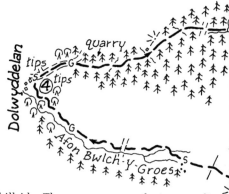

DESCRIPTION An 8¾ mile walk for experienced hill walkers exploring the forest and open hills between Penmachno and Dolwyddelan, returning by historic Tŷ Mawr (See Walk 8 for details). After an initial climb north from Penmachno the walk heads west following an old route through the forest, rising in easy stages to Bwlch y Groes (1410 feet/430 metres), then descending to the edge of Dolwyddelan. The route then returns via forest and open ground, later descending to Tŷ Mawr in the attractive Wybrnant valley, before a final section of attractive upland road – formerly a drovers' route. Allow about 5½ hours. The route can be shortened to a 6 mile walk from Tŷ Mawr. Note that sections of this walk can become muddy after rain.
START The Eagles, Penmachno [SH 790506]

1 From The Eagles take the side road signposted to Tŷ Mawr. Almost immediately turn RIGHT along a side road, past an imposing chapel and on to cross a bridge over the river. At the end of Ty'n-y ddol angle LEFT along a track then continue up a driveway, past a turning to Dolydd. On the bend cross a ladder-stile ahead and go up the steep slope to the forest corner above. Follow an enclosed path up to cross a stream and stile beyond, then continue up to a forestry track above. Follow it LEFT through the forest, later rising beneath a cottage to a crossroad of tracks. Go up the track ahead. When it levels out and splits follow the track ahead. At the next junction turn LEFT to reach a minor road. Turn RIGHT up the road, signposted to Tŷ Mawr.

2 On the next bend by a yellow grit container take a stony path on the left through trees, soon crossed by a mountain bike trail. Continue on the now green path through the forest, later bending RIGHT across a stream and rising gently. Shortly, the path bends LEFT up onto the more open

hillside. The now narrow path rises steadily up the heather/bilberry covered slope – *with extensive views south east to distant Llantisilio Mountains and south to Carnedd y Filiast and Arenig Fach.* When the path fades continue up the high ground ahead, soon levelling out with a small heather/bilberry knoll to your left and a good view of Moel Siabod. Here angle RIGHT down to go through a large gap in an old wall by the corner of mature trees.

3 Now follow a clear path – *briefly enjoying new mountain views* – soon passing through a narrow clearing to a small gateway in the wall. The path now rises in stages through the forest, crossing three streams. After passing through a more open section of forest and a final wettish reedy area you leave the forest by a stile at Bwlch y Groes. Turn LEFT alongside the fence and past a small gate in the forest corner. The path now heads down heather/reedy terrain towards Dolwyddelan, with its castle prominent in the valley below – *enjoying good views of Moel Siabod and other mountains.* The path descends a more reedy area and becomes indistinct. Continue down towards Dolwyddelan, through a gap in an old wall, then descend the reedy and tussocky hillside to a stile in a fence to join a green track. The track meanders down the hillside, following the course of the Afon Bwlch-y-Groes past the nearby forest, later crossing a forestry road. Continue down the old track, flirting with the river, to eventually reach a ladder-stile/gate near a house on the edge of Dolwyddelan.

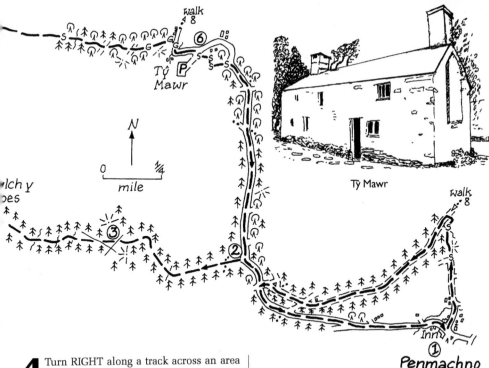

Tŷ Mawr

Penmachno

4 Turn RIGHT along a track across an area of quarry spoil heaps to a gate into a forest. Immediately take a waymarked footpath on the right up through trees, initially on an old quarry incline. After passing the top of the tree-covered old quarry the path levels out, continues to a stream, then rises to a waymark post at a fenced corner of the forest. Follow the waymarked path ahead over the stream and along the forest edge – *enjoying good views*. The path then enters the forest, crosses a stream and continues to a waymark post, after which it begins to rise. After crossing another stream the path bends right and rises steadily through the forest, crosses a forestry road and continues up to a stile at the forest perimeter.

5 The path crosses tussocky/reedy open ground, soon passing to the left of an old stone wall. The variable path then rises through heather, crosses wettish reedy ground, and continues past a waymark post to a ladder-stile into the forest. Follow the path down to a forestry track, then down the open woodland – *with a view into the Wybrnant valley* – to an older forestry track. Take a path opposite signposted to Tŷ Mawr down the open tree-covered slope – *soon with a view down to TŷMawr* – to a gate/stile. Follow the path between walls then down a field edge towards a house. Go through a gate on the right and down to join a minor road below. Follow it RIGHT through a gate and on over the river to reach the entrance to Tŷ Mawr. Continue up the narrow road.

6 At the entrance to the road leading to Tŷ Mawr car park, cross a stile. Go up the field edge to another stile, then turn RIGHT up the edge of a reedy field to a further stile. Turn LEFT along the field edge to stiles to rejoin the road. The road rises steadily, eventually levelling out and passing an open aspect – *with views to Moel Pen-y-bryn and distant Arenig Fach beyond*. The road passes forestry tracks then reaches your outward route. Now simply follow the road down through the forest and along Cwm Glasgwm back to Penmachno.

WALK 8
TŶ MAWR

DESCRIPTION A 7½ mile undulating walk on a scenic minor road, forestry tracks and paths, providing an opportunity to visit the remote upland historic house of Tŷ Mawr, now owned by the National Trust [*open Easter–Oct Thur–Sun 12.00–17.00. Charge*]. The walk follows a minor road, formerly a drovers' route, up through an area of forest and down to Tŷ Mawr, before continuing along and down the attractive Wybrnant valley. After a choice of continuing road then forestry track (**route a**) or undulating path (**route b**) it goes along the wooded edge of the Lledr valley, then climbs through the forest and heads back to Penmachno. Allow about 4½ hours.

START The Eagles, Penmachno [SH 790506].

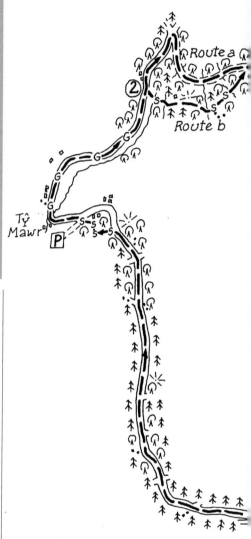

*T*ŷ *Mawr, meaning 'Big House', is the birthplace in 1545 of William Morgan, who later became Bishop of St Asaph. His achievement of translating the bible into Welsh is regarded as a major milestone in the history of the language. Inside the house is a display of Welsh bibles, including Morgan's 1588 bible. Although situated in the now remote Wybrnant valley this typical 16thC farmhouse and other nearby were on a once important old drovers' route from Anglesey to Mid-Wales.*

From The Eagles go along the minor road signposted to Tŷ Mawr. After crossing the Afon Glasgwm continue along the road, soon rising – *with a good view along the part -forested Glasgwm valley and across to the bare top of Moel-Pen-y-bryn.* When the road splits go up the right fork signposted to Tŷ Mawr. The narrow road – *part of an old drovers' route from Dolwyddelan via Penmachno to Ysbyty Ifan* – climbs steadily through the forest, eventually levelling out. Shortly, the road begins to descend, passes forestry tracks – *with a good view of Moel Siabod* – then descends more steeply – *soon with a view into the wooded Wybrnant valley.* On the bend cross two stiles on the left and follow the fence to cross a stile in the

corner. Follow the wall/fence down through reeds to cross another stile at the corner of a small wood. Descend the field edge to a stile onto the access road for Tŷ Mawr's car park. Rejoin the nearby road and follow it down to Tŷ Mawr. After visiting the ancient house continue along the gated road, over the river and on past Pwll y Garth. The narrow attractive upland road briefly accompanies the river, then descends steadily into the wooded valley.

12

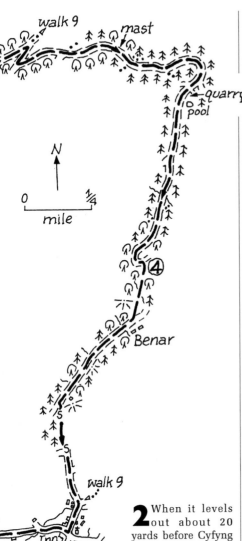

embankment just ahead then turn left down a wide walled path to a stile. Follow the path down through the trees to a stony forestry track where you join the main walk at point 3.)For **Route a** continue past Cyfyng – and descend the road in stages to where a forestry track crosses. Here turn sharp RIGHT along the stony track through an area of deciduous woodland and over the river by a small waterfall. After passing a turning area the track climbs steadily to where it is crossed by a waymarked path. Here you are joined by Route b.

3 Continue up the forestry track through mature deciduous trees. At a track junction do a sharp U-turn RIGHT and follow the track up to another junction. Here do a sharp U-turn LEFT and continue up the track – *soon enjoying extensive views across the wooded Lledr valley and west to Moel Siabod, the Glyders, Tryfan and Carneddau mountains.* When the track bends sharp right keep ahead up a narrower stony track, shortly passing a telephone mast, then a waymarked cross path and bike trail. Later the track bends south and levels out. At a track junction keep ahead past other side tracks and a quarry area containing a small pool and on through the forest. When it splits go down the left fork, briefly joined by a bike trail, then passing through a part cleared area of forest.

4 About 15 yards after the track bends sharp left take a waymarked path angling back on the right, soon descending through attractive mature deciduous trees to cross a stream. The path continues down the part wooded hillside – *with a view down into the Machno valley* – to join another forestry track above 17thC Benar. Follow it RIGHT, soon passing through mature trees, then an area of cleared forest with a small stone ruin below on your left – *with a good view down to Penmachno.* About 70 yards beyond the ruin go down a wide path on the left to cross a stile and a stream. Follow the enclosed path down beside the forest, then descend the steep slope to a ladder-stile onto a driveway. Follow it down to Ty'n-y ddol and continue along the road to Penmachno.

2 When it levels out about 20 yards before Cyfyng – *a former school* – you have a choice. (For **Route b** take a waymarked path on the right down through bracken and small trees to cross two footbridges over the river and a stile beyond. Follow the path left through trees to a waymark post. After crossing a stream the path bears left through the wood and on above a moss covered stone ruin, then descends to cross a footbridge over a stream. The path now rises through trees to a stile. Cross the

MACHNO FALLS & ROMAN BRIDGE

DESCRIPTION A 7 mile walk (**A**) exploring the wooded hillside and valleys north of Penmachno. The walk follows paths and forestry tracks, later descending by a choice of routes to a minor road near the meeting of the Conwy and Lledr valleys. It follows the road past the Conwy gorge and Machno Falls to an ancient packhorse bridge, then returns along the Machno valley. An alternative 5¾ mile walk (**B**) is included.
START The Eagles, Penmachno [SH 790506].

From The Eagles take the side road signposted to Tŷ Mawr. Almost immediately turn RIGHT along a side road, past an imposing 19thC chapel and on to cross a bridge over the river. At the end of Ty'n-y ddol angle LEFT along a track then continue up a driveway, past a turning to Dolydd. On the bend cross a ladder-stile ahead and go up the steep slope to the forest corner above. Follow an enclosed path up to cross a stream and stile, then continue up to a forestry track above. Follow it RIGHT, then after ⅓ mile, with 17thC Benar visible just below, go up a waymarked path on the left. It rises across reedy/bracken covered terrain, crosses a stream, then continues up through trees to a stony forestry track. Turn LEFT up the track, later being briefly joined by a mountain bike trail. At a junction keep ahead, soon rising and continuing past side tracks at a quarry area containing a pool. Keep ahead, now on a narrower forestry track, soon descending and bending west. Go past another waymarked bike trail, descending steadily.

2 Shortly you reach a bike trail on the right and a waymarked cross path. (For **Walk B** turn right and follow the path down through conifers, shortly bending right across a stream and continuing across the dense conifer covered slope down to another

stream. The path continues through deciduous woodland, later shared with a bike trail. When the level stony path bends half-right follow a less distinct path ahead past a green forestry warning board. Follow the path through mixed part open woodland to a stile/gate. Go across the small clearing and past a substantial old house. Continue along its green access track, through a large clearing to gates onto a stony forestry track. Follow it left. At a junction, turn sharp right down the track to join the main route at point **4**, or to visit the packhorse bridge follow the track ahead down to the valley road.)

For **Walk A** continue down the track past a large telephone mast and through an open area of mixed woodland – *offering a good view down into the wooded Lledr valley and to Moel Siabod, then the Glyders, Tryfan and the Carneddau mountains.* Just beyond a barrier gate and before the bend of another track you have a choice of descent routes to the valley road. (For **Route b** do a sharp U-turn RIGHT on a waymarked path/permitted bridleway. Follow the improving path down through mixed open woodland.) For **Route a** continue down the track, then do a sharp U-turn RIGHT down another stony track, soon joined by another, later passing above houses to reach a minor road. Turn RIGHT up the road.

3 Follow the valley road above the river Conwy, dominated by Dinas Mawr – *which George Borrow described as 'an immense mountain' in his famous book 'Wild Wales', when he walked beneath it in 1854.* Later you pass a viewpoint of the Conwy gorge to reach Pandy Mill. *Opposite its garage a path leads down past the ruined corn mill to Machno Falls.* Continue along the road, past a forestry road, to reach a bridge over the Afon Machno. *Just downstream is the 17thC packhorse bridge, known as 'Roman Bridge'. Nearby is the former Penmachno Woollen Mill, built originally in the 1830s as a fulling mill.* Return a few yards then take a path on the left before a finger post up through the trees. After a few yards bear LEFT up to a point above the river opposite the former woollen mill.

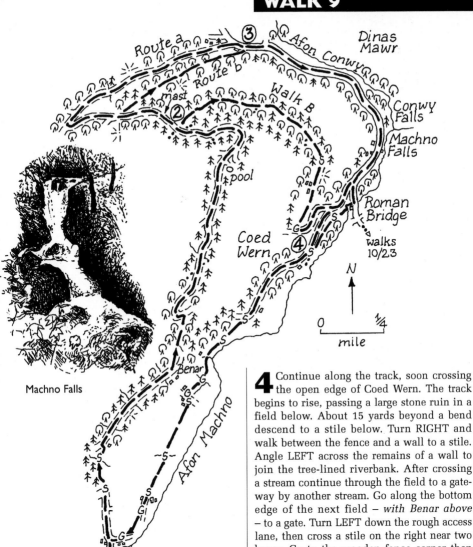

Dinas Mawr

Route a

Route b

mast

Walk B

Conwy Falls

Machno Falls

pool

Coed Wern

Roman Bridge

walks 10/23

N

0   ¼

mile

Machno Falls

Benar

Afon Machno

walk 10

Penmachno

4 Continue along the track, soon crossing the open edge of Coed Wern. The track begins to rise, passing a large stone ruin in a field below. About 15 yards beyond a bend descend to a stile below. Turn RIGHT and walk between the fence and a wall to a stile. Angle LEFT across the remains of a wall to join the tree-lined riverbank. After crossing a stream continue through the field to a gateway by another stream. Go along the bottom edge of the next field – *with Benar above* – to a gate. Turn LEFT down the rough access lane, then cross a stile on the right near two barns. Go to the wooden fence corner then along the large field to a sleeper bridge and ladder-stile in the boundary ahead. Go across the middle of the next field, through a large gap in the hedge/tree boundary, then across a further field to a ladder-stile/gate by an old farm. Go past the house and barn and briefly along its green access track, then go through a kissing gate on the right. Go along the edge of the large field to a wooden gate in the corner to rejoin the access track. Follow it RIGHT to join your outward route by Ty'n-y ddol.

Descend the path and follow it through the edge of woodland to a stile. Continue on the path between an old moss covered wall and a fence to reach two stiles. Cross the one on the right to join the forestry track just above. Turn LEFT.

15

LOWER MACHNO VALLEY

DESCRIPTION A 4¾ mile walk around the lower Machno valley. The route first follows field paths along the western side of the valley, then goes along the edge of Coed Wern to an ancient packhorse bridge by the former Penmachno Woollen Mill. It then returns along higher upland pasture on the more open eastern side of the valley, enjoying extensive views. Allow about 3½ hours.

START War memorial/Churchyard, Penmachno [SH 790505].

*S*t *Tudclud's church is reputed to be the burial site of Iorwerth ab Owain Gwynedd (1145-74), the father of the Welsh prince Llywelyn the Great.*

I Go along the road to The Eagles, then take the side road signposted to Ty Mawr. Almost immediately turn RIGHT along a side road, past an imposing 19thC chapel and on to cross a bridge over the river. At the end of Ty'n-y ddol turn RIGHT along a track to a facing gate. Here go through a small wooden gate on the left and continue along the field edge to a kissing gate. Follow the green access track to pass through an old farm to a ladder-stile. Keep ahead across two fields to a ladder-stile and sleeper bridge, then continue across the next large field. Go past a facing gate by two barns, then turn LEFT to a stile. Go up the stony track then just before a cattle grid take a waymarked path through a gate on the right. Go along the bottom field edge and through a gateway. Continue through the next field, over a stream then near the river. Just before a facing gate ahead angle LEFT to cross an old wall and a stile beyond. Continue between the perimeter fence of the wood and a wall, then cross a stile on the left to join a forestry track above. Follow it RIGHT along the open edge of Coed Wern, later becoming enclosed by trees.

2 After a further 100 yards, just before the track rises and bends left, descend to a stile down to your right, adjoining another. After crossing the stile follow a path LEFT beside the fence along the wood edge to another stile. Continue with the path through woodland, soon near the river and rising to a good view across to the former woollen mill, after which it descends to a minor road. Turn RIGHT to the bridge over the Afon Penmachno. *Just downstream is the 17thC stone packhorse bridge, known as 'Roman Bridge'.* Follow the road past the former Penmachno Woollen Mill – *built originally in the 1830s as a water powered fulling mill* – and houses to the B4406. Go up the minor road opposite.

3 After about 25 yards cross a stile on the right. Angle LEFT through bracken and along the edge of a wettish reedy area to another stile. Follow the path up the bracken-covered slope, very soon bending RIGHT up through trees to a waymark post and a stile above. Continue through reeds then bracken up to the field corner, where there are two waymarked paths. Take the one through a gate on the right, then turn LEFT up the field edge to a stile/gate. Continue near the fence up the edge of the bracken/reedy terrain to pass just to the left of a small tree-covered rocky knoll. Now angle away from the fence to pass a large tree/waymark post in a reedy area ahead and on to go through a gate in the boundary, where the path splits. Take the waymarked (red dot) path on the right through bracken and go across the field aiming to the left of a tree-covered ridge ahead. Go through a gap in the bracken-covered wall boundary and keep ahead, with the tree-covered knoll to your right, to cross a stream in the corner and go through a gate beyond. Go up the slope ahead to join an access lane. Follow it RIGHT up to Bryn Eithin and go past a barn (gates).

4 Just beyond the end of the house, turn RIGHT through a gate between the house and an outbuilding to pass an old water pump and go through a gateway. Angle LEFT to follow a rough green track near the boundary to a ladder-stile/gate. Go across the field – *enjoying good views of the mountains ahead* – to a stile/gate. Continue across the

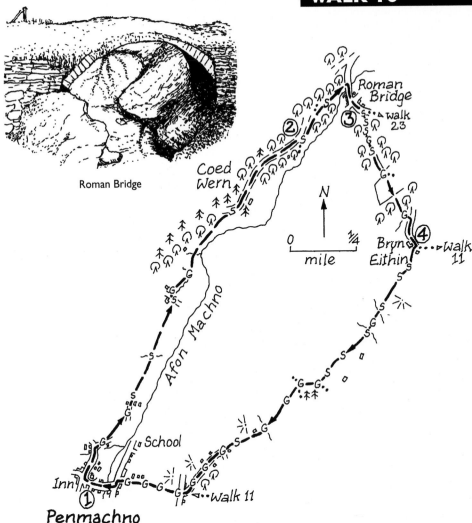

Roman Bridge

Penmachno

next large field to another stile/gate. Cross the stream and angle LEFT across tussocky ground to join the fence on your left, then go through a waymarked gate ahead in the corner. Continue beside the wall, over a stone slab bridge then a stile. Follow the wall on your right through three fields then go through a gate in the corner where you join a green track. Follow the track past a small plantation to a gate. Cross a farm track then follow a narrow old gated walled track ahead up to its end. Go past the ruin ahead – *with a view down to Penmachno* – pass through

two wall gaps, then follow the wall on your right down to a stile. Follow the path to pass an outbuilding and the front of Rhos y Mawn to a small gate, then go along the access track ahead down to a gate by a cottage. Continue down the track – *enjoying good views* – to another gate by terraced cottages and on to a minor road. Go through a kissing gate opposite and follow the enclosed stony path down through further kissing gates to the main road in Penmachno. Follow it LEFT, bending past the former Machno Inn and over the river to the start.

HWYLFA

DESCRIPTION A 6 mile walk (**A**) exploring an area of upland pasture and woodland NE of Penmachno, offering extensive views. The route rises in stages to Coed Maen Bleddyn then follows a waymarked path across rougher terrain up to the ruin of Hwylfa, and a great viewpoint (1148 feet/350 metres), before descending in stages to Penmachno. A lower alternative 3¾ mile walk (**B**) is included.
START War memorial/Church, Penmachno [SH 790505].

I Follow the road over the river and past the former Machno Inn. Bend LEFT with the main road then take a signposted path between terraced houses on the right to a kissing gate. Follow the enclosed path up the hillside through further kissing gates to a minor road. Follow it LEFT. When it bends down left go up the access track ahead, past cottages and Ty hir fuches goch and on to a gate by another cottage. Go along the green track then cross a stile ahead. Follow the wall on your left up beneath a house to its driveway. After a nearby cattle grid, angle RIGHT up the field to a gate on the skyline. Follow the old tree boundary to a farm track then turn RIGHT a few yards to a nearby small iron gate. Keep ahead to follow a fence through a tussocky/reedy field. At the fence corner continue ahead, shortly crossing a small gorse-covered rise to cross a footbridge over the Nant Caddugan and a nearby stile. Angle slightly RIGHT, soon crossing higher ground past trees to a fence corner. Go along the edge of a large reedy field to a farm track by a stile/gate. Follow it RIGHT to another stile/gate, then continue along the track. After a stream the track fades in line with a nearby stile/gate on the left. (For **Walk B** turn right then angle left up past a small ruin to a stile/gate into Open Access land. Keep ahead, then bear right on a path/quad track up the gorse/bracken covered hillside. Soon head to a nearby post on your right onto a small rise. Follow a path towards a small craggy top ahead, then up to a stile. Pass

below high ground ahead to join the main walk at a stream at point **5**.)

2 Cross the stile and go across the field to a ladder-stile, then follow a rough green track to a gateway at the rear of Bryn Eithin by an old water pump. Go through a gate between the house and an outbuilding, then turn RIGHT. Follow the waymarked path through another gate, then after crossing the stream angle sharp LEFT across the field towards a small tree-covered ridge to a stile. Keep ahead on the signposted red dot path across reedy ground then up the field to a gate in the corner. Now bear LEFT moving away from the wall across tussocky ground to a visible waymark post ahead, then continue through gorse to a kissing gate into Coed Maen Bleddyn. Follow a faint green track through the mature woodland, soon descending to a more distinct cross-track. Follow it RIGHT to a gate at the wood edge. Continue along the old green track.

3 After about 120 yards, when the track bears left, turn RIGHT to follow a path up between streams to a stile/gate. After a few yards bear RIGHT alongside the fence up to go through a gate in it and another on the left. Follow the signed path up the reedy/bracken slope, very soon bearing LEFT past a post and continuing across the bracken/part-wooded slope, past another post to cross a stream and a ladder-stile beyond. Continue across a more open area of bracken and gorse – *enjoying extensive views east*. Pass to the right of a post, after which the path soon rises to another, then continues across a reedy area to cross a stream. Continue with the path a little way from the stream, shortly crossing it just before a wall. Bear RIGHT alongside the wall to cross a ladder-stile. Turn RIGHT and follow the wall up the hillside to a stile. Follow the signed red dot path up across tussocky ground to a waymark post at the end of the ruin of Hwylfa ahead – *a good place to stop to enjoy the panoramic views*.

School

Penmachno

4 Go past the front of the ruin, then bear RIGHT to pass through an old wall. Continue with the old embanked wall just to your right and past old workings on your left, then follow a quad track up the slope on your right. When it fades continue towards the wall ahead, then just before it follow a path LEFT to reach a waymark post at the old wall ahead – *a great viewpoint looking down into Cwm*

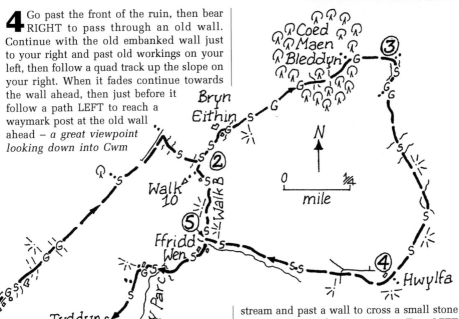

stream and past a wall to cross a small stone slab bridge over the Nant y Parc. Turn LEFT up a green track to a stile/gate. Go ahead up the field then turn LEFT in front of the cottage to a small gate. Turn LEFT then RIGHT past the end of the cottage to a gate, then go along its green access track. As it bends right go through a waymarked gate ahead and across the field to a stile. Follow the boundary up the field to a ladder-stile. Go up the field towards Tyddyn uchaf, through a gate and across a paddock to another gate just beyond stables, then two further gates onto its access track. [For the security of horses please leave gates as you find them, and beware of a Burmese cat joining your walk!] Continue along the track.

Penmachno, with a panorama of mountains beyond. Continue ahead down the part gorse/bracken covered slope past a waymark post to cross two stiles in the bottom left-hand corner. Keep ahead down the rough upland pasture following a nearby stream and old wall on the left guided by waymark posts. After a third post by the stream continue along the old embanked wall and on through bracken and gorse to a stile in a fence. Continue near the stream down to a post at a cross-path. Turn LEFT.

5 Cross the stream and follow the path to pass behind the ruined farmhouse of Ffridd Wen. At its far end angle RIGHT down the slope to an old gateway and on to a way-marked stile ahead. Follow the boundary LEFT round to a gap in the wall then follow the rough path down and on along the old embanked field edge. Bear RIGHT across a

6 Just beyond where the track is crossed by electricity cables (a small gate may be installed here) angle up to a ruin, go along its shelf, then angle RIGHT up past the far end of a wall to join an access track beyond. Follow it RIGHT down to a cottage, then a path round its right hand end to a stile amongst shrubs. Go down the field to a ladder-stile in the bottom left-hand corner. Now follow the stiled path down the edge of three fields to the minor road. Return down your outward route.

Y FOEL

DESCRIPTION A meandering figure of eight 4 mile (**A**) or 3½ mile (**B**) walk exploring the network of paths above Penmachno, offering extensive views. The route rises in stages by a choice of routes across upland pasture to Y Foel (918 feet/280 metres). It then descends and heads via historic Hafod Dwyryd to a delightful crossing of the Afon Machno, before returning to Penmachno. Allow about 3 hours. The route can easily be undertaken as two shorter walks using the road as shown.

START War memorial/Church, Penmachno [SH 790505] or Coed Pen-y-bryn [SH 787498].

I Follow the road over the river and past the former Machno Inn. Bend left with the main road, then take a signposted path between terraced houses on the right to a kissing gate. Follow the enclosed path up to a minor road. Follow it LEFT. When it bends down left go up the access track ahead, past cottages to a gate by another. Go along the track. (For **Walk B** cross a stile ahead. Follow the wall on your left up beneath a house to its driveway. After a nearby cattle grid, turn right up the field edge to go through a gate in the corner. Turn left up the edge of a long field to a ladder-stile. Continue up the edge of two further fields to cross a ladder-stile on the skyline ahead. Follow the fence right up to a stile in it to join Walk A then resume instructions in paragraph **3**.)

2 For **Walk A** follow the stony track up to a house. Go through a small iron gate into its garden, then go past its gable end and through another gate. Turn LEFT up alongside an old wall, then go through a gap in it at a bank of gorse. Go along the top field edge, past a wall corner, and up to a ladder-stile. Follow the wall on your right along the edge of rough pasture soon between walls to cross a ladder-stile. Head to the front of a nearby ruin – *offering a good view down to Penmachno and along Cwm Glasgwm* – then follow a faint green track across the hillside and continue past Rhos

y Mawn to a small wooden gate in the fence onto an access track. Follow it up to another cottage. Follow its perimeter fence round to a stile/gate then cross a ladder-stile beyond. Turn LEFT behind the cottage and up to a stile. Continue beside the wall across rough pasture, then about 15 yards before a second intersecting wall, angle RIGHT across a wide gap in the adjoining ridge and on to a stile ahead. Turn RIGHT.

3 Follow the the fence-topped embanked boundary up the rough pasture then across Y Foel – *enjoying extensive views* – and down to a gate onto an access track. (For **Walk B** turn right then angle up to a ruin. Go along its shelf, then angle right up past the far end of a wall onto an access lane to rejoin Walk A at point **4**.) For **Walk A** go along the green track ahead to a stile/gates, then turn RIGHT alongside the fence. Ignore the old embanked boundary but continue beside a wall to a lane. Follow it RIGHT past a nearby house, then turn RIGHT along an access track, crossing a cattle grid. Follow it up past a house, then just beyond another cattle grid turn LEFT up an access lane.

4 At the top cross a stile by a gate and go along the right hand side of an old wall ahead past a stone ruin. At its corner turn LEFT over a low wall, then follow the wall on your left to a wide gap in the wall corner. Keep ahead down the slope then follow a path angling RIGHT down the hillside. At its end continue down past a telegraph pole (3B) to the right hand end of an old wall. Cross a stile below then go down the field edge to Foel. Pass between the house and an outbuilding, then follow its access track to a minor road. Go down the road.

5 Shortly cross a stile up on the left opposite Swch y Llan. Follow the fence to cross an old wall ahead, then bear RIGHT to a small wooden gate near the end of the cottage. Go down the edge of the reedy field to cross a footbridge over the Nant y Mynach. Turn RIGHT above the stream down to cross a stile. Angle RIGHT down the field towards a distant barn, through the old tree boundary and on across the reedy terrain. About

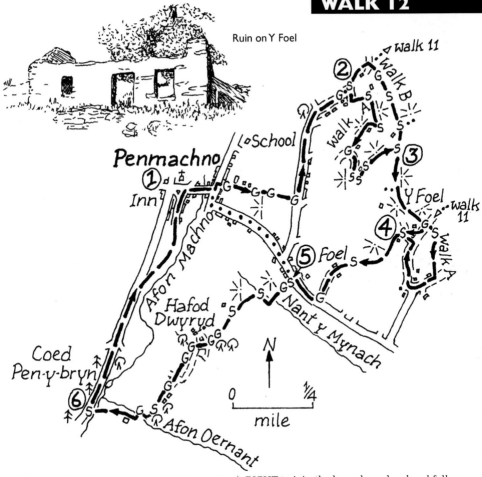

Ruin on Y Foel

Penmachno

Inn

Hafod Dwyryd

Coed Pen-y-bryn

Afon Machno

Nant y Mynach

Y Foel

Foel

Afon Oernant

N

0   ¼

mile

50 yards before the barn turn LEFT to a stile in the fence/tree boundary. Keep ahead, then angle down to a gate in the wall on your right before the field corner. Follow the track down to another gate and a stony track beyond. Follow it RIGHT towards Hafod Deg – *a 16thC manor house* – then go along a track on the left. When it bends down towards buildings follow the fence on your left to cross a bridge over a stream and go through a gate beyond. Continue to another nearby gate, then along an old green track. Cross the bend of the adjoining stony track and go along the access track ahead. Go through the gated entrance to Cae Gwyn and past the front of the cottage, then continue through young trees to a stile/gate. Angle

RIGHT to join the boundary ahead and follow it to a kissing gate, then cross a footbridge over the Afon Oernant. Turn RIGHT alongside the river past an elaborate stone barn then head to a large footbridge over the Afon Machno – *a great place to stop*. Continue to a ladder-stile onto the road.

6 Follow it RIGHT past the entrance to Coed Pen-y-bryn (alternative start). About 150 yards further take a hedge-lined path angling down on the right, soon near the river and passing stepping stones over it. The path then moves away from the river to join a lane which continues past houses in Penmachno to the main road.

OERNANT

DESCRIPTION A 5½ mile (**A**), 4¾ mile (**B**), or 3½ mile (**C**) walk exploring a varied landscape of river valley, enclosed upland pasture, Open Access land, and forest near Penmachno, offering extensive views. The route heads south along the Machno valley then rises across open upland pasture to cross the delightful Afon Oernant. Walk C returns by forestry road and field paths. The main route meanders through a forest then crosses the edge of more Open Access land. Walk B then continues by road and track. Walk A passes through a recently cleared forest offering panoramic views before descending into a hidden upland valley. Both routes then combine on a descent through enclosed upland pasture to Penmachno. Allow about 4 hours. Please note that the Afon Oernant may be more difficult to cross after heavy rain.

START War memorial/Church, Penmachno [SH 790505] or Coed Pen-y-bryn [SH 787498].

1 Go along the nearby no through road (White Street) by the elaborate bus shelter. Follow it past an old chapel and houses, then continue along an enclosed path, soon joining the river near stepping stones. Follow the path up to the road, then continue along its right hand side, soon reaching the entrance to Coed Pen-y-bryn (alternative start).

2 Follow the road southwards along the Machno valley. Shortly cross a ladder-stile on the left then a nearby footbridge over the river. Angle slightly RIGHT to the end of a wall and past a telegraph pole beyond, then continue along the top edge of a reedy area to a gate. Go along the next field edge to another gate, then continue along a green track. When it angles right keep ahead, past a telegraph pole and on across the bank edge of the field up to pass the end of a wall. Keep ahead – *with a good view along the upper Machno valley to the former slate quarries* – to a gate into a tiny fenced enclosure above the river. Go through a small gate in its left hand corner into a gated sheep pen. Turn

LEFT through the large gate then a facing gate ahead. Continue up to a waymark post at a large field corner.

3 Go up the field edge above a narrow old walled way then go through a waymarked gate in the wall. Turn LEFT and follow the wall to a stream then up the edge of rough upland pasture. At its end go through the right of two facing gates into Open Access land. Continue with a rough path about 10 yards from the fence across the tussocky/reedy terrain. Later join the fence to pass above a small wooded gorge, down which the Afon Oernant tumbles. Cross a shallow section of the river to a wooden gate opposite and follow the waymarked path through conifers to a nearby forestry track. Follow it LEFT past a horse arena – *created in 2005 by local volunteers* – to the bend of a forestry road by an information board. (For **Walk C** go down the forestry road ahead to a stone stile/gates, then down past a stone ruin at a good viewpoint. When it bends left follow a track to a gate ahead and over a stream. After a few yards, with Hafod Deg – *a 16thC manor house* – ahead, turn right up a short gated track into a field. Bear LEFT, rising away from the wall, then continue to a stile in the boundary ahead. After 15 yards angle right up through reeds and an old tree boundary, then up to a stile above the Nant y Mynach. Turn right along its bank to cross a footbridge over it. Go up the reedy field edge to go through a small wooden gate on the right just before a cottage. Just beyond bear LEFT across an old wall and on to a stile onto a road. Follow it down into Penmachno.)

4 Turn RIGHT along the forestry road. At a junction turn RIGHT up to another junction. Turn LEFT, soon bending right, after which the forestry road begins to rise steadily. At a turning area with a yellow bridle trail waymark post, turn LEFT to a nearby stile/gate into open country. Keep ahead across the rough upland pasture to join a narrow track which runs along the forest edge and continues towards Pen-y-ffridd. After a gate continue through the farm then along its access track to the road. (For **Walk B** go down the road then along a minor road

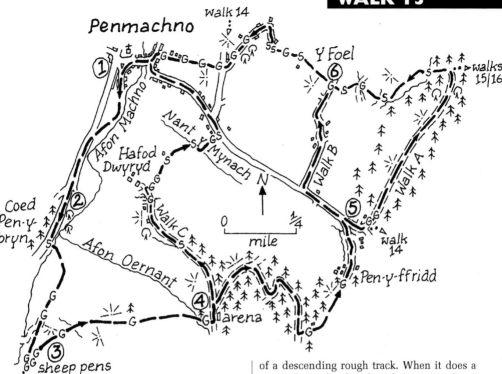

on the right. Just beyond a house turn left over a cattle grid and follow an access track up past another house. After another cattle grid at a junction continue ahead to rejoin the main route at point **6**.)

5 For **Walk A** do a sharp U-turn up a stony access track, then take its gated left fork past a house into the nearby forest. Follow the track across the cleared forest – *enjoying panoramic views* – soon rising steadily, then levelling out. After a turning area the track narrows. At another turning area with a bench seat turn LEFT down a waymarked path through trees and up to a stile into open country. Go to the left of an old embanked boundary ahead to the remains of a stone structure on it. Here turn LEFT and head across the edge of a tussocky area beneath high ground. Keep ahead, past the forest fence corner up to your left, down the slope – *with a small lake visible below*. Descend the reedy/tussocky terrain almost parallel with the forest fence above to join the end

of a descending rough track. When it does a U-turn keep ahead and work your way down to a ladder-stile below near a gate at the forest corner. Head down the field to a small wooden gate in the fence corner to join an access lane beyond. Turn LEFT then after a few yards, when it bends left, continue ahead across open ground to a stile by gates. Go along the short track to a nearby access track.

6 Go through the gate opposite and up the left hand field edge, then continue with the fence-topped embanked boundary across the tussocky ground of Y Foel – *enjoying extensive views*. Shortly, go through a wide gap in the old boundary to a nearby stile. Follow the field edge down to a small wooden gate in the corner. Go past the rock slab ahead to a good viewpoint down to Penmachno, then descend to a ladder-stile by a cottage and a stile/gate beyond. Follow its access track down past other cottages to a minor road. Go through a kissing gate opposite and follow the enclosed path down to the main road in Penmachno. Follow it LEFT, soon crossing the river, back to the start.

RHIW LWYD

DESCRIPTION A 5¾ mile walk for experienced hill walkers exploring an attractive upland Open Access area to the east of Penmachno, offering breathtaking all-round views. From Penmachno the walk follows an old drovers' route, initially a narrow road then stony track, south-east up into open country to a bwlch overlooking Cwm Eidda. From here it heads across nearby high ground to a trig point on Rhiw Lwyd (1305 feet/398 metres), then crosses short tussocky upland pasture visiting several small rocky tops, before descending a waymarked path to a ruined farm. It then returns across upland farmland. Allow about 4 hours.
START War memorial/Churchyard, Penmachno [SH 790505].

I Follow the road over the river and on the bend by the former Machno Inn turn RIGHT along a minor road, soon bending left and rising steadily south east away from the village. Eventually it becomes two stony tracks. Go up the left one. When it splits take the right fork for a few yards then go through a gate ahead into an old walled track on the waymarked red horse trail at the edge of open country. The narrow stony track rises steadily alongside the boundary across tussocky/reedy terrain – *offering a good view west to Cwm Penmachno and its old slate quarries, and looking back over Penmachno to a panorama of mountains.* The track eventually levels out at the bwlch with new views, then descends gently to a ladder-stile/gate – *offering extensive views across the wild upland pasture grazed by sheep and black cattle, as the old drovers' route continues into Cwm Eidda and down to Ysbyty Ifan.* Return up the track.

2 Where it levels out turn RIGHT onto nearby high ground. Go across the flattish top of Bryn Llech, soon with a trig point visible ahead. Continue across the broad tussocky ridge to a stile in a fence, then up to the trig point on Rhiw Lwyd. The views are breathtaking for such a low top – *east-*

wards to Mynydd Hiraethog, then clockwise to the distant Llantisilio Mountains, the bare hills above Ysbyty Ifan, the Arenigs, distant Moelwyns, Snowdon, Moel Siabod, Tryfan, Glyders the Carneddau range and north along the Conwy valley to the coast. Angle LEFT to cross a stile in the nearby fence, then continue beside it. When the fence angles right continue a few yards from it across the upland pasture grazed by sheep and horses. After skirting a wet reedy area continue parallel with the fence, then angle away to climb onto the small rocky top ahead. Descend its northern side to a wall below and follow it LEFT. After about 15 yards cross a stone stile in the wall.

3 Pass to the left of the small top just ahead then follow a sketchy path across the mid-slopes just beneath the rocky ridge, soon bending slightly right. When it fades continue down a tussocky area passing to the left of another rocky crag. At the bottom of the slope angle LEFT on a faint quad track across wettish/tussocky ground – *to your right can be seen a stile in a fence* – and on up the part gorse-covered ridge ahead to pass across its left hand shoulder. Keep ahead passing just beneath the short ridge's rocky top. After a very brief descent go onto higher ground just ahead, then continue down the small tussocky ridge to join an old wall ahead. Follow it LEFT then after a few yards go through a wide gap in it. Continue with the wall to pass through a small reedy area to cross two stiles to join a waymarked public footpath.

4 Continue ahead down the part gorse covered tussocky/reedy upland pasture following a nearby stream and old wall on the left guided by occasional waymark posts with red circle. After a third post by the stream and old wall corner continue along the old embanked wall and on through bracken and gorse to cross a stile in a fence ahead. Continue near the stream down to a post at a cross-path. Turn LEFT across the stream and follow the path to pass behind the ruined farmhouse of Ffridd Wen. At its far end angle

School

Penmachno

Inn

①

RIGHT down the reedy slope to an old gateway and on to a waymarked stile ahead. Follow the boundary LEFT round to a gap in the wall then follow the rough path down and on along the old embanked field edge. Bear RIGHT across a stream and past a wall to cross a small stone slab bridge across the Nant y Parc. Turn LEFT up a green track to a stile/gate. Go ahead up the field towards a cottage, then just before its fence corner turn RIGHT across the field, through a waymarked gap in a wall

and on past a ruin, then down to a stile in the bottom left-hand field corner. Cross a stone slab bridge over the Nant Caddugan and go through a waymarked gate.

5 Turn LEFT along the edge of the large field, later crossing a stile and footbridge over the Nant Caddugan. Keep ahead gently rising through bracken and follow a faint path across the tussocky/reedy ground to reach a fence corner. Follow the fence to a small iron gate onto a farm track. Go along the right hand side of the old tree boundary opposite to a gate – *offering a good view*

down to Penmachno. Descend the field to an access track leading to a nearby house. After the cattle grid follow the wall on your right down beneath the house and on to a stile. Follow the access track to a nearby gate by a cottage and on past further cottages, then go up a road. After ¼ mile go through a kissing gate on the right by a telephone box. Follow the delightful enclosed stony path down through further kissing gates towards Penmachno to emerge onto the village road.

PENMACHNO TO CWM EIDDA

DESCRIPTION A 7½ mile walk from Penmachno to Cwm Eidda for experienced hill walkers, offering extensive views. The route climbs in stages into open rough upland pasture, crosses a broad ridge (1148 feet/350 metres), then descends to a minor road in Cwm Eidda. From Eidda Fawr farm you have a choice of routes up to the bwlch, before a splendid descent on an old drovers' road to Penmachno. **Route a** follows a waymarked path across rough upland pasture. **Route b** continues along the road to join the old drovers' road earlier. Allow about 5 hours.

START War memorial/Churchyard, Penmachno [SH 790505].

I Follow the road over the river and past the former Machno Inn. Bend left with the main road bends, then take a signposted path on the right between terraced houses to a kissing gate. Follow the enclosed stony path up to a minor road. Go to the track opposite, then cross a stile up on the right. Go up the field edge to a ladder-stile. At a waymarked telegraph pole ahead angle LEFT up the field to a ladder-stile and continue up to a stile/gate by a cottage. Go past the end of the cottage to a ladder-stile. Go up the slope ahead and on to a small waymarked gate in the corner. Go up the field edge to a stile and through a gap in the boundary beyond. Turn RIGHT and follow the fenced topped embanked boundary across the tussocky upland pasture of Y Foel – *enjoying extensive views* – and down to a gate onto an access track. Go along a green track opposite to a stile.

2 Follow the fence on your left to join an access lane. After crossing the stream turn RIGHT to a nearby small wooden gate. Head up the field to a ladder-stile in its right hand corner. Angle LEFT up the slope, then go up a short farm track. Continue up the reedy/tussocky terrain, soon passing about 40 yards below the forest perimeter fence

corner, then go across the right hand edge of a flattish area beneath high ground. At the remains of a stone structure turn RIGHT past the short embanked boundary up to a stile into the forest. Turn LEFT, soon bending RIGHT and rising through trees to reach a waymark post at the bend of a forestry track, with a bench seat nearby. Keep ahead along the narrowing green track to a small gate into open country. Angle LEFT across the part reedy covered terrain, soon rising across the gorse covered slope to a stone stile in the wall ahead.

3 Cross the stile and keep ahead to pass along the base of the small gorse-covered slope, then follow the path across the tussocky terrain towards a rocky hillock. When it fades angle RIGHT up and across the tussocky ground, then along the right hand edge of flattish ground, passing beneath rocky crags and high ground. Continue across a tussocky/reedy area to a stile in a fence. Keep ahead along the edge of reedy terrain, gradually descending on an intermittent path across a wettish reedy area, then go up green pasture ahead. Now, with a gate ahead, angle RIGHT to a stile in the fence visible on the skyline. Continue down the next field to a stile between strips of woodland. Cross the small ridge ahead, descend to another stile and cross the stream. Angle RIGHT across the field to a stile and descend the next field – *enjoying good views into Cwm Eidda* – to a stile/gate in the bottom left-hand corner. Turn LEFT down the field edge to a waymarked gate. Go down the field to a stile/gate by a stream. Continue down the edge of the next two fields onto a minor road. Follow it RIGHT along Cwm Eidda past Ty Uchaf to reach Eidda Fawr farm. (For **Route b** continue along the road, then when it bends left to Pont Blaen-Eidda turn right up a rough track. Follow it to cross Pont Rhyd-yr-halen, then up across rough pasture to point **5**.)

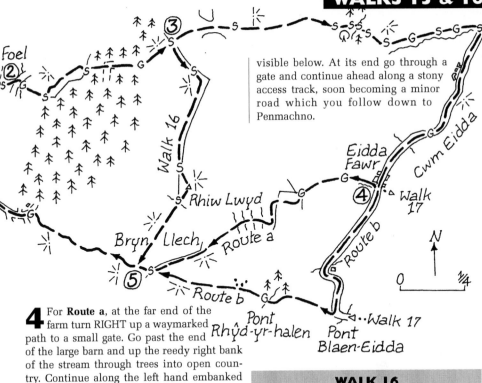

visible below. At its end go through a gate and continue ahead along a stony access track, soon becoming a minor road which you follow down to Penmachno.

4 For **Route a**, at the far end of the farm turn RIGHT up a waymarked path to a small gate. Go past the end of the large barn and up the reedy right bank of the stream through trees into open country. Continue along the left hand embanked edge of a sunken reedy track to a facing gate by a ruin. Continue beside the fence above the old track up into rough upland pasture. After a gate keep ahead beside the wall to a gate in it, then turn RIGHT across the tussocky ground to a waymark post on an old embanked boundary. Walk LEFT along the old boundary, then after about 200 yards, as it begins a gentle descent, follow a clear path leading RIGHT towards the distant trig point on Rhiw Lwyd. It then heads to a visible waymark post and continues across the tussocky terrain up to another post on the skyline at a good viewpoint. Keep ahead past a waymark post at the fence corner, then follow the fence across tussocky ground to a ladder-stile/gate to join a green track at the bwlch. Go up the track, soon levelling out – *enjoying extensive views of Snowdon and other mountains, and along Cwm Penmachno.*

5 The track – *part of an old drovers' route from Anglesey via Penmachno and Ysbyty Ifan to Mid-Wales* – now steadily descends towards Penmachno, shortly

WALK 16
RHIW LWYD

DESCRIPTION A 4¼ mile walk (**B**) for experienced hill walkers, rising in stages to a broad ridge of Open Access land featuring Rhiw Lwyd (1305 feet/398 metres), offering panoramic views and returning down an old drovers' route. Allow about 3 hours.
START As Walk 15.

1-2 Follow instructions in paragraphs 1 & 2 of Walk 15.

3 Follow the wall up past a higher stone stile onto a small rocky top offering all-round views. Descend to follow the nearby fence south across the rough upland pasture to cross a stile in it, then angle RIGHT to the trig point on Rhiw Lwyd. Descend south to a stile then continue across the broad tussocky ridge, then the flattish top of Bryn Llech to join a track at the bwlch. Follow instructions in paragraph 5 of Walk 15.

27

CWM EIDDA

DESCRIPTION A 5 mile (**A**) walk, offering extensive views, exploring the attractive upland pasture around Cwm Eidda, with its working farms. The walk first follows part of an old drovers' road across upland pasture, linking the two communities of Ysbyty Ifan and Penmachno, along which men once brought cattle from Anglesey to Mid-Wales. After reaching the bwlch at 1280 feet/390 metres, it follows a waymarked path across rougher pasture into Cwm Eidda, then rises in stages before a final descent to Ysbyty Ifan. Allow about 3½ hours. Equally enjoyable shorter alternative 3 mile (**B**), 2 mile (**C**) and 1¾ mile (**D**) walks are included. **START** Ysbyty Ifan [SH 842488].

*T*he *Knights of St John*, who established the hospice here, became renowned for their hospitality, receiving privileges from both Welsh Princes and English kings, including the rights of sanctuary for their tenants and protection in Royal Courts. After being destroyed by fire around 1400 during Owain Glyndwr's rebellion against English rule the hospice was rebuilt. Later it was taken over by outlaws who abused the rights of protection. After years of lawlessness in the area which included robbery, murder and cattle stealing, they were forced out in the early 16thC. In 1540 Henry VIII banned the Order of St John as part of his dissolution of monasteries and the hospice became a ruin. The current Victorian St John's church was built where the hospice and original church once stood. Its graveyard contains graves of many dignitaries. Today the spirit of the Knights of St John lives on through the well known St John Ambulance Association.

I From the car parking area above the river return to the B4407. Turn LEFT past Ffynnon Penrhyn, then RIGHT up a side road past the Almshouses – *rebuilt in the 19thC to replace original almshouses established here in 1700 for six 'poor aged men'.* The road rises steadily. When it bends right to a house go up a stony tree-lined track ahead to a gate.

Continue up the track to another gate and on up to a minor road. Turn RIGHT up the road, soon levelling out – *offering panoramic views towards Moel Siabod, the Glyders, Tryfan, the Carneddau Range and along the Conwy valley.* (For **Walk D**, just before the access track to Foel Gopyn, turn sharp right and follow a gated green track, then embankment to join the returning main walk at a waymark post.) Continue along the road. (For **Walk C** head right to a small gate at the end of conifers, then follow the stiled path through two fields to join the returning main walk just before a wall.) After passing another road on the right, the narrow scenic upland road begins a long steady descent across upland pasture – *with views into Cwm Eidda.* (Later, for **Walk B** take a signposted path through a gate on the right, and go across three fields to join the main walk at point **4**.)

2 After passing through a gate the road continues to cross Pont Blaen-Eidda, a tall single arched stone bridge over the Afon Eidda. When the road bends right keep ahead up a rough track (signed 'unsuitable for motors') beside the wall. Follow it past a small plantation to cross Pont Rhyd-yr-halen and through a gate into Open Access land. The track now rises steadily across reed and gorse-covered pasture to reach a ladder-stile/gate just below the bwlch. Continue briefly up the track for extensive views into Cwm Penmachno and of a panorama of mountains, including Snowdon. Return to cross the ladder-stile, then turn LEFT.

3 Follow the fence across the tussocky ground, then at the fence corner, follow the waymarked path ahead to another post. Continue on an improving path in the same direction down the upland pasture towards a gate in a distant wall, to another waymark post. After crossing a stream, the path bends slightly right and crosses further streams to reach an old embanked field boundary. Follow it LEFT round to a waymark post on the embankment at a gap in it. Turn RIGHT and head towards the gate in the wall (your earlier target) then turn LEFT to go through

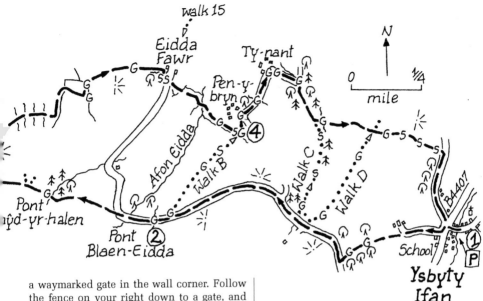

a waymarked gate in the wall corner. Follow the fence on your right down to a gate, and continue down the embanked edge of an old reedy track. After a post work your way down the left hand edge of the old track/stream. Just before the barn corner at Eidda Fawr, follow the signed alternative stiled path down to the road. Turn RIGHT, then after a few yards, LEFT to follow the signposted path down the edge of a field and round to cross a footbridge over the Afon Eidda. Follow the waymarked path up to a gate in the top right hand field corner, and up the next field edge above a stream to cross a stile. Follow the fence LEFT round to go through a gate.

4 Follow the enclosed waymarked path down to a gate at Pen-y-bryn farm. Continue along the nearby narrow gated road

to Ty-nant, where the road bends right and rises. When it bends left go through the facing gate ahead. Turn RIGHT along the rough farm track and follow it up through the reedy field. After passing through an old wall, turn LEFT down through a gateway and over a stream. Follow the faint track up across reedy ground, shortly alongside an old wall/embankment to reach a waymark post on another old embanked boundary. Keep ahead across reedy ground to a kissing gate in the boundary corner. Descend the edge of three fields – *enjoying extensive views along the Conwy valley and south west to the Arenigs* – to a wood corner to join the road below. Follow it down to Ysbyty Ifan.

About the author, David Berry

David is an experienced walker with a love of the countryside and an interest in local history. He is the author of a series of walks guidebooks covering North Wales, where he has lived and worked for many years. He has worked as a Rights of Way surveyor across North Wales and served as a member of Denbighshire Local Access Forum.

Whether on a riverside ramble, mountain or long distance walk, he greatly appreciates the beauty, culture and history of the landscape and hopes that his comprehensive guidebooks will encourage people to explore on foot its diverse scenery and rich heritage.

PONT RHYDLANFAIR

DESCRIPTION A 7 mile walk exploring attractive undulating enclosed upland pasture to the north of Ysbyty Ifan, offering good mountain views, using quiet country roads, tracks and available paths. The walk first rises from Ysbyty Ifan then descends via Pant Glas to the A5, where it crosses the delightful wooded Conwy gorge hidden from passing motorists. After following a scenic upland road along the north side of the valley it descends again to the A5 (with a roadside tea bar). Here it recrosses the Conwy river by the splendid ancient stone bridge of Pont Rhydlanfair and returns across the edge of Cwm Eidda. Allow about 4 hours.
START Ysbyty Ifan [SH 842488].

1 Return to the B4407 and go up the minor road opposite signposted to Cwm Eidda – *soon with a good view looking down over Ysbyty Ifan* – past a small wood and a signposted path (your return route). Eventually the road levels out at a bend – *offering superb all-round views. To the north west is a panorama of mountains, including Moel Siabod, Snowdon, the Glyders, Tryfan and the Carneddau range. To the east is the expansive Mynydd Hiraethog. To the south is the long bare ridge leading to Carnedd y Filiast, with the Arenigs beyond.* Go through the gate ahead and along Ochr Cefn Isaf's rough access lane, shortly beginning a steady descent. When it bends right continue ahead down a track – *enjoying good views north along the Conwy Valley* – through a gate and on past a wood. Continue with the track past the entrance to Gwernovau and through a gate beyond. Soon angle down a green track past a barn to Pant Glas. (Alternatively continue down the main access track to the A5.) *The present house was converted from stables, using stone from the original house which was built as the home for the Vaughan family 400 years ago.* Go past the house, then turn LEFT towards outbuildings then RIGHT to a gate at their end. Go down the field edge

to a small gate onto the A5. Turn LEFT along the pavement.

2 At its end cross with care to the minor road opposite. Cross Pont Rhyd-y-Dyfrgi (1862) over the wooded Conwy gorge then go up the road – *later enjoying good mountain views.* At a junction by a wood turn LEFT and follow the road down to cross over the river and up to a house, then a farm. Continue along the road to pass a graveyard, chapel and cottages, then take a signposted path through a large iron kissing gate on the left. Follow the fence and stream down the field to a stile, then continue down a small wooded valley to a kissing gate, then stile. Go down the field edge, then after about 25 yards angle away from the fence down the field to cross a gated footbridge over a stream. Cross the stony track and head up the field to a set of gates onto the nearby road. Follow the road LEFT past Rhydlanfair farm and down to the A5. (In a lay-by a 100 yards to the right is a tea bar.)

3 Take the minor road opposite to cross the stylish 18thC single arched stone bridge of Pont Rhydlanfair over the river Conwy. Continue up the road past a side road and follow the road south east – *with good views across the valley to your outward route.* Follow the road past a farm, the entrance to Bryn Glas, Fron Ddu and Pen-y-geulan. Go past a road on the right then on the next bend go down a rough track past a cottage and over the river. Cross a raised stile ahead, then go up a depression in the field to an old wall. Follow the old embanked boundary left up to a stile/gate. Go up the next field to a gate in the corner, then turn LEFT up a road, soon passing a side road. It continues to rise steadily, offering good views west.

4 Just before you reach the bend of the road and your outward route, take a signposted path through a gate set back on the right. Follow the old enclosed green track, later sunken and reedy, up to a gate. Continue along the embankment above the old reedy track to reach a waymark post just beyond a wall corner. Here turn LEFT across reedy ground to a kissing gate in the boundary corner. Descend the field edge to a stile, then continue down the next – *enjoying extensive views along the Conwy valley and south west to the Arenigs* – to a stile/gate. Descend the next field edge to another stile/gate at a wood corner to rejoin the road below. Follow it down to Ysbyty Ifan.

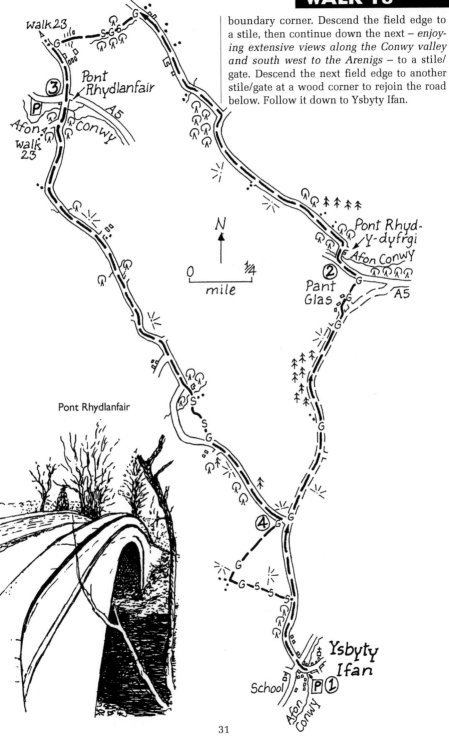

Pont Rhydlanfair

WALK 19
CWM CALETWR

DESCRIPTION A 3¾ mile walk exploring enclosed upland pasture to the east of Ysbyty Ifan, with extensive views. The route follows field paths and scenic upland roads to a remote farm, then heads north on tracks and field paths along the edge of the Caletwr valley before returning by road. Allow about 2½ hours.
START Ysbyty Ifan [SH 842488].

1 From the car parking area above the river follow the road through the village. Soon, take a minor road on the right between houses and up into open country. Just before a junction by a cemetery and an old chapel go through a kissing gate on the left. Go along the field edge to another kissing gate, then follow the wall up the next field to a further kissing gate and cross a footbridge over the stream beyond. Continue up the edge of three further fields and on to a minor road. Turn RIGHT up the road. At a junction, turn LEFT and follow the road past a nearby farm and on down to Cerrigellgwm Isaf farm.

2 Go past the house and at the small corrugated building ahead bear LEFT through a gateway, then immediately RIGHT to cross a concrete footbridge over the river. Turn LEFT along the field edge to a gate, then turn RIGHT along a track. After fording the Nant Llan-gwrach continue along the track, over a stream and through the gate beyond. Go up the track, through another gate and on past a small stone ruin, soon bending right. When the track bends left to a gate go through a facing gate ahead then turn LEFT along an old sunken track to a gate. Continue along the green track. When it bends right follow the embanked fence on your left down to cross a fence and a stream below. At the fence corner beyond turn LEFT above the stream to cross a ladder-stile (due to be installed) in the corner. Continue northwards beside the wall, shortly descending the long field to a gap in the bottom corner. Keep ahead beneath high ground and down the field towards houses to go through a gateway in the wall on your right. Angle LEFT to a stile then follow a path between buildings to the road. Turn LEFT and follow the scenic undulating road back to Ysbyty Ifan.

WALK 20
BWLCH BLAEN-Y-CWM

DESCRIPTION A 9½ mile walk exploring a little known upland area lying to the east of Ysbyty Ifan, offering panoramic views. The route rises in stages by field paths and scenic road to a farm at the edge of an expansive upland landscape. After crossing a river the route follows a good track up another river valley, then across open country up to Bwlch Blaen-y-cwm (1407 feet/429 metres). After descending a byway into Cwm Ceirw it follows narrow scenic roads along the valley then north up and across upland pasture past Garn Prys. After a steady descent the route follows a bridleway to the historic 16thC Gilar then an old drovers' road and scenic road back to Ysbyty Ifan. Allow about 5½ hours.
START Ysbyty Ifan [SH 842488].

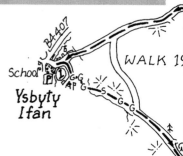

1 Follow instructions in paragraph **1** of Walk 19.

2 Go past the house and to the right of a small corrugated building to ford the river to join a track beyond. (If river is high use concrete footbridge just downstream.) Follow the track past deciduous woodland into open country, then ford the Nant Llan-gwrach or cross it just downstream. The gated track now rises steadily, later becoming sunken in nature, eventually bending to a gate at Bwlch Blaen-y-cwm, where it levels out.

3 Follow the part tarmaced old road down the valley to reach the bend of the access road leading down to Blaen-y-cwm farm. Go up the narrow road and follow it along the edge of Cwm Ceirw to a junction. Follow the road up to another junction. Here turn LEFT up past Tyn Bwlch then follow the road beneath the eastern slopes of Garn Prys. The road then bends north east and begins a long steady descent, later passing Hafotty-bach.

4 About 100 yards beyond, at a finger post, turn LEFT along a farm track. Follow the track to a gate by outbuildings then between walls to another gate into a large field. Continue ahead beside the wall, shortly descending to go through a small then large gate at the corner of a conifer plantation.

Follow the wall down the plantation/field edge and go through a gateway in the field corner. Continue on a green track across the edge of a reedy area to a gate into a field. Go along the field edge past a wood. At its corner turn LEFT through a gate, then follow a track to Gilar. *This traditional 17thC Welsh manor house was once the home of poet Rhys Wynn and the Price family, descended from Cardinal Wolsey's cross-bearer.* Go through a facing gate and another gate in the right hand corner by stone outbuildings. Go past the end of the barn, then follow a farm track past the nearby gatehouse (*1623*) to join Gilar's access lane.

5 On the bend go through a small way-marked (Mynydd Hiraethog) iron gate by a finger post. Now follow a delightful old enclosed gated green drovers' road which skirts the small hill of Bryn Prys, later descending and joining a more defined access track to reach a road. Follow it LEFT for 1½ miles to Ysbyty Ifan.

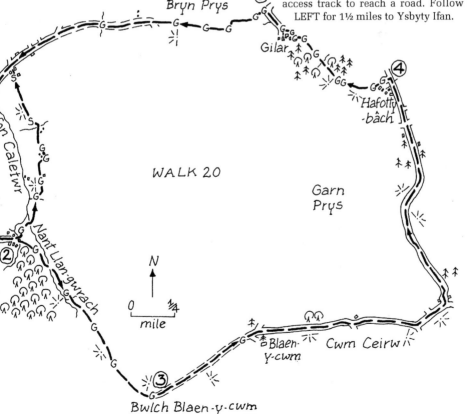

Bryn Prys

Gilar

Hafotty-bach

WALK 20

Garn Prys

Nant Llan-gwrach

N

0   ¼
mile

Blaen-y-cwm

Cwm Ceirw

Bwlch Blaen-y-cwm

CEFN GWYN

DESCRIPTION An exhilarating 8¼ mile walk around the contrasting upper Conwy valley, featuring a little known hidden wild upland landscape and great views. The route follows a lane then green track – an old drovers' route – south into open country to its end. It then heads on intermittent paths across tussocky/reedy Open Access land and up across the shoulder of Cefn Gwyn (1378 feet/420 metres). After a long steady descent the route crosses the Afon Serw by stepping stones then the Conwy gorge to join the B4407. The return route follows good paths up across enclosed upland pasture on the northern side of the Conwy valley, then descends to Ysbyty Ifan. *This walk is for experienced, well equipped, hill walkers, and should be avoided in poor visibility and after heavy rain when the Afon Serw may be in spate.* Allow about 5 hours.

START Ysbyty Ifan [SH 842488].

I From the car park above the river follow the road through the village. Soon, take a minor road on the right between houses and up to a junction by a cemetery and nearby old chapel. Continue up the narrow road to its end at Ty'n-y-ffridd. Follow the signposted path ahead along a rough track to a gate, then continue up the old sunken track to another gate. The reedy track now rises into open country to a ladder-stile/gate, then continues up and across the wild upland landscape – *offering extensive mountain views, including Arenig Fach ahead.* After a gate the track continues towards the Arenigs then descends into the Nant Adwyr-llan valley. After a ladder-stile/gate the track continues along the edge of the reedy valley then bends left and passes stone sheepfolds to end at a stile/gate beyond a stream.

2 Cross the stile and turn sharp RIGHT to follow the fence down to the stream near the corner of the sheepfolds. Here turn LEFT and follow a path through reeds and up the tussocky slope ahead. Continue with the path towards Arenig Fach, rising gently.

When in line with the fence corner below, the path bends and contours across the tussocky hillside. Keep with the main path parallel with the fence about 100 yards below, soon following a quad track through a rougher area. When in line with the remote cottage of Cefngwyn, angle RIGHT down to cross the fence where it intersects with another. Follow the other fence (on your right) to join a nearby stream. After a few yards cross it and continue by the fence. Ahead lies the top of Cefn Gwyn, your next objective. From the fence corner work your way across tussocky ground, over a stream where it joins another. Follow a path along its right bank, passing a boulder. At a narrow wettish reedy area follow it RIGHT up tussocky ground, then continue up a reedy grass embankment to reach the a small stone ruin beneath the ridge – *a good place to stop.* Continue up the small embankment to cross a fence where it is joined by another. Follow the embankment up over the eastern shoulder of Cefn Gwyn then go through a gate in the fence to your left.

3 Go along a faint quad track parallel with the nearby fence. Shortly the fence angles away as you begin to descend towards Moel Trwyn-swch – *with a great view along remote Cwm Serw* – to the right of the old embanked boundary, then on beside a reedy stream to a gate. Continue on the old embanked path above the stream. The path soon angles away from the stream, before continuing more or less parallel with it. The path then makes a long gentle descent along the right hand edge of a reedy area. Eventually you reach a track by the ford of the Afon Serw. Cross the river by stepping stones and go along the track. Shortly, turn RIGHT along a green track to a gate. Continue up the old reedy track, then just before it bends up to an old long Welsh farmhouse turn RIGHT along the right embanked edge of an old reedy sunken path. Cross to the other side where

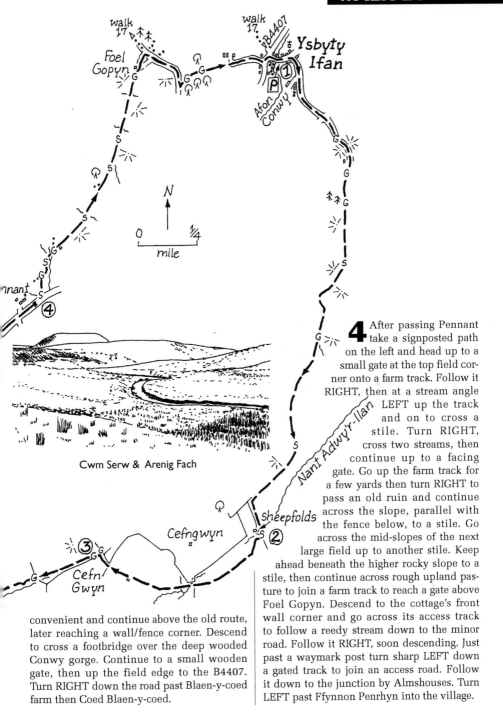

Cwm Serw & Arenig Fach

4 After passing Pennant take a signposted path on the left and head up to a small gate at the top field corner onto a farm track. Follow it RIGHT, then at a stream angle LEFT up the track and on to cross a stile. Turn RIGHT, cross two streams, then continue up to a facing gate. Go up the farm track for a few yards then turn RIGHT to pass an old ruin and continue across the slope, parallel with the fence below, to a stile. Go across the mid-slopes of the next large field up to another stile. Keep ahead beneath the higher rocky slope to a stile, then continue across rough upland pasture to join a farm track to reach a gate above Foel Gopyn. Descend to the cottage's front wall corner and go across its access track to follow a reedy stream down to the minor road. Follow it RIGHT, soon descending. Just past a waymark post turn sharp LEFT down a gated track to join an access road. Follow it down to the junction by Almshouses. Turn LEFT past Ffynnon Penrhyn into the village.

convenient and continue above the old route, later reaching a wall/fence corner. Descend to cross a footbridge over the deep wooded Conwy gorge. Continue to a small wooden gate, then up the field edge to the B4407. Turn RIGHT down the road past Blaen-y-coed farm then Coed Blaen-y-coed.

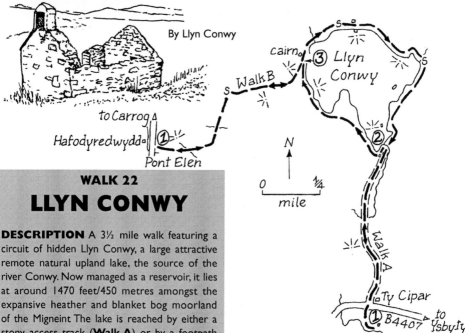

LLYN CONWY

DESCRIPTION A 3½ mile walk featuring a circuit of hidden Llyn Conwy, a large attractive remote natural upland lake, the source of the river Conwy. Now managed as a reservoir, it lies at around 1470 feet/450 metres amongst the expansive heather and blanket bog moorland of the Migneint The lake is reached by either a stony access track (**Walk A**) or by a footpath (**Walk B**). The clockwise lake circuit, which follows intermittent paths through predominantly rough heather terrain, is for experienced hill walkers and should be avoided in poor visibility. Walk A includes a visit to nearby delightful waterfalls. Allow about 2½ hours.
START Ty Cipar [SH 781446] or
Pont Elen [SH 765457].
DIRECTIONS Ty Cipar lies on the B4407, 5 miles from Ysbyty Ifan. Pont Ellen lies on a minor road accessible from both the B4407 and Carrog in the Penmachno valley.

1 For **Walk A** first head south across open ground down to visit the waterfalls on the Afon Conwy, then return. From Ty Cipar follow the stony track north across the vast heather moorland to eventually reach Llyn Conwy near a boathouse.

2 Head south to the nearby small ruined dwelling – *once used overnight by fishermen* – then follow a faint path along the western edge of the lake. After about 250 yards the path angles away from the lake and crosses high ground ahead, passing a small stone structure to your left. The faint path continues down to the lake then close along

its edge. Shortly head up to a nearby old waymark post below a stone cairn to join a better path.

3 Follow the path around the lake's north western corner to a ladder-stile, then to an old boathouse. Continue near the rocky shore and on to a stile at its north eastern corner. Go along the lake's eastern side past a nearby small island, after which a path continues a little way from the lake, then bends to a handrailed footbridge. Continue to the stony access track.

Walk B

I Follow the signposted path up the rough open pasture near the boundary. Just before a fence corner the path bears LEFT, crosses a stream/ reedy area, then continues up near the fence to a ladder-stile. Angle RIGHT then follow a gently rising path, vague in places, eastwards. Shortly the path bends north-eastwards and descends towards Llyn Conwy to an old waymark post below a stone cairn. Now follow instructions in paragraphs **3** and **2** of Walk A to complete a circuit of the lake.

CONWY FALLS

DESCRIPTION A 4¼ mile walk around a little known area of the Conwy valley, offering good views, combined with a visit to Conwy Falls (small payment) and home made refreshments in the cafe designed by William Clough-Ellis who built Portmeirion. After visiting the Falls and an ancient packhorse bridge, the route then follows a scenic narrow country road to cross the Afon Conwy by Pont Rhydlanfair, a splendid single-arched 18thC stone bridge. The return route crosses upland farmland on the northern side of the valley before descending another scenic minor road. Allow about 3 hours.
START Conwy Falls cafe [SH 811535].
DIRECTIONS The café and large car park is at the junction of the A5/B4406. Walkers are welcome.

to cross Pont Rhydlanfair to reach the A5. (A lay-by tea bar is 100 yards to the left.)

2 Go up the road opposite past Rhydlanfair farm then on the bend turn LEFT up the access track to Bancog farm. Just beyond the house go through a gate on the right by an outbuilding and go up the slope. Follow the fence on your left, then cross a gated stone stile ahead and stream to reach a gate by a small outbuilding at Carreg-coediog farm. (The Right of Way follows the track ahead through the farm and up the hillside.) To follow an alternative permissive waymarked National Trust path that avoids the farm, at the gate turn RIGHT and follow the fence up the hillside. At its corner angle LEFT to follow cables, pass between gorse and go across open ground to join the farm track at a gate. Follow the track to a nearby stone barn then go through a gate ahead into a field. Angle RIGHT across the large field to a kissing gate in the boundary ahead. Continue in the same direction across the next large field, then midway bear LEFT to a gate ahead.

3 Go across the next field towards Penrhyddion Pella to another gate. Continue along the next field edge and through a large gate beneath the house and a small metal gate ahead below an outbuilding. Just beyond turn RIGHT up a path through gorse and round

1 Follow the circular path through woodland overlooking Conwy Falls. Afterwards, follow the B4406 down to cross the river and continue for ½ mile to minor crossroads. First turn RIGHT past cottages to the former Penmachno Woollen Mill – *built originally in the 1830s as a water powered fulling mill. Just downstream is the single arched 17thC packhorse bridge, known as the 'Roman Bridge'.* Return to the crossroads and continue up the narrow road opposite. Follow it for 1⅓ miles to a junction and down

to a small wooden gate. Go along the edge of a parking area to the nearby minor road. Follow it LEFT, soon descending between Penrhyddion Canol and Penrhyddion Uchaf farm. Continue down this narrow scenic gated road to the A5. Cross the road with care to reach the nearby junction and café.

WALK 24
CARNEDD Y FILIAST

DESCRIPTION A 8½ mile walk for experienced hill walkers featuring a mountain top and a long ridge dominating the skyline south of Isbyty Ifan, with panoramic views throughout. Starting from Llyn Celyn the route follows a meandering track for 3½ miles up across heather moorland to Carnedd y Filiast (2194 feet/669 metres). It then follows a path alongside a fence west along the wide open tussocky/heather ridge descending in stages to join an old drovers' way heading south. You then have a choice of routes. **Walk A** continues on a gradual descent across upland pasture. **Walk B** follows an attractive stream down into Cwm Gelyn then returns along a minor valley road. Allow about 5½ hours and avoid in poor visibility.

START Parking area by Llyn Celyn [SH 858411].

DIRECTIONS From Fron Goch follow the A4212 west past the National Whitewater Centre, past a car park by the dam of Llyn Celyn. Continue along the wooded side of Llyn Celyn past three further car parks to find a car park at an open aspect of the lake.

Llyn Celyn reservoir was built between 1960-65 to provide water for Liverpool. The flooding of Tryweryn Valley and Capel Celyn village, a strong Welsh speaking community containing farms, houses, a school, chapel, cemetery and post office, was highly controversial and provoked widespread opposition throughout Wales. It remains a sad chapter in modern Welsh history.

I Walk east along the roadside verge adjoining the wooded edge of the lake. Shortly, take a wide stony track opposite angling back up through the forest. At a turning area go up the narrow green track ahead, soon angling RIGHT on a waymarked bridleway up a stony track to a stile/gate at the forest perimeter into Open Access land.

Continue up the old track rising steadily across the bilberry/heather terrain – *enjoying views across the expansive Migneint to the Snowdonia mountains.* The track continues across the heather moorland, later rising steadily towards Foel-boeth, then bending east across its southern slopes – *enjoying extensive views south* – and descending to a track junction.

2 Here turn LEFT, soon descending towards Cwm Hesgyn, with Llyn Hesgyn visible at its head. After crossing the Nant y Coed the track rises steadily across the heather covered eastern flanks of Brottos, then bends away from the Hesgyn valley, rising more steeply. Eventually the track levels out and briefly becomes a path before continuing across Carnedd y Filiast's eastern shoulder, then bending up to reach a cairn and sheltered trig point on its summit – *offering panoramic all-round views.*

3 Now follow a path alongside the fence westwards down and across the wild tussocky part heather covered terrain, later rising to a ladder-stile/fence, then continuing up to a small stone cairn on Carnedd Llechwedd-llyfn. The path and fence now descend an initial stone covered slope then continue across the heather/tussocky terrain, passing a joining fence on your right, crossing a stream, then passing a slate boundary marker (1866–RP). After crossing a fence you reach another joining fence on the right.

38

Carnedd
Llechwedd-llyfn

Carnedd
y Filiast

4 Continue ahead alongside the ridge fence past another slate boundary stone, then join a quad track which follows the fence down to reach a stile/ old gate in it. Here you are joined by the old drovers' route from Ysbyty Ifan. Turn LEFT across the reedy/tussocky ground, soon joining a quad track, which runs parallel with the fence about 70 yards to your right, then descends towards Llyn Celyn. As you approach the fence corner, the quad track angles left to cross the Nant-goch. Go up the short reedy rise ahead.

Brottos

Nant-y-Coed

Foel-boeth

N

0   ¼
mile

5 For **Walk A** angle RIGHT through reeds to join a quad track. After a few yards, as it angles down right, keep ahead on a sketchy path across the rock strewn upland pasture towards Llyn Celyn, gently descending, then continue parallel with a wall below to a gate in a fence ahead. Keep ahead then angle down towards the wall and follow a path above it down to a stile. Continue parallel with the wall/ fence through reeds, soon descending to cross a stream. A few yards beyond angle LEFT on a path up to join a green track. Follow it across reedy terrain to join the nearby wall/fence. After a gate the track continues past outbuildings to another gate ahead. Just beyond, at the fenced sheepfold corner keep ahead, soon joining a green track. Follow it

across open pasture and down to a small stone building near a wall. Cross a stream and continue above the wall down to a stile/gate to join an old road and Walk B just ahead.

For **Walk B** turn RIGHT and follow the delightful Nant-goch down towards the valley, passing above an old stone structure to join an old green track which passes through a wall boundary by sheepfolds. Follow the track down through a reedy area and on to a gate in a fence corner. The green track continues towards conifers then angles LEFT across a reedy area. At a fence corner turn RIGHT to a ladder-stile at the entrance to Craignant. Follow the minor road along the Gelyn valley. Later, when the road bends right down to the A4212, follow an old road to a nearby gate ahead and on to other gates where you are joined by Walk A. Continue along the old road to a gate, then descend through trees to cross the A4212 and follow it back to the start.

An alternative 9¼ mile walk, for experienced hill walkers, to Carnedd-y-Filiast can be made from Ysbyty Ifan. Follow instructions in paragraphs **1** and **2** of Walk 20 to Bwlch Blaen-y-cwm, where a gate allows entry to Open Access land. Head south east, at first on a good path, up the hillside onto the broad ridge. Follow it south west up across Waun Garnedd-y-filiast to the trig point on Carnedd-y-Filiast. Now follow instructions in paragraph **3** of Walk 24 westwards along the ridge. At point **4** cross the ridge fence and follow the joining fence northwards down the hillside, later above the Nant y Fuddai, to a stile/gate, with sheepfolds nearby (point **2** of Walk 21). Join a green track beyond and follow it across the wild upland landscape to Ty'n-y-ffridd, then a narrow road down to Ysbyty Ifan.

PRONUNCIATION

Welsh	English equivalent
c	always hard, as in **cat**
ch	as in the Scottish word lo**ch**
dd	as th in **then**
f	as f in o**f**
ff	as ff in o**ff**
g	always hard as in **got**
ll	no real equivalent. It is like 'th' in then, but with an 'L' sound added to it, giving 'thlan' for the pronunciation of the Welsh 'Llan'.

In Welsh the accent usually falls on the last-but-one syllable of a word.

KEY TO THE MAPS

- **--→** Walk route and direction
- Metalled road
- Unsurfaced road
- **. . . .** Footpath/route adjoining walk route
- River/stream
- Trees
- Railway
- **G** Gate
- **S** Stile
- **F.B.** Footbridge
- Viewpoint
- **P** Parking
- **T** Telephone

THE COUNTRYSIDE CODE

- Be safe – plan ahead and follow any signs
- Leave gates and property as you find them
- Protect plants and animals, and take your litter home
- Keep dogs under close control
- Consider other people

Open Access
Some routes cross areas of land where walkers have the legal right of access under The CRoW Act 2000 introduced in May 2005. Access can be subject to restrictions and closure for land management or safety reasons for up to 28 days a year. Please respect any notices. The Countryside Council for Wales website (www.ccw.gov.uk) provides updated information on any closures.

Acknowledgements
Special thanks to Ioan Davies, Area Warden, Snowdonia National Park Authority for his co-operation and efforts in upgrading the extensive network of paths around Penmachno with the installation of stiles and gates. Also thanks to Andrew Roberts, National Trust Warden and Conwy Borough Council Rights of Way Section.

Right of Way problems
Contact Conwy County Borough Council Countryside Service and Rights of Way section [Tel 01492 574000 or via www.conwy.gov.uk] regarding any problems encountered.

Published by **Kittiwake**
3 Glantwymyn Village Workshops, Glantwymyn, Machynlleth, Montgomeryshire SY20 8LY
© Text & map research: David Berry 2011
© Maps & illustrations: Kittiwake 2011
Drawings by Morag Perrott
Cover photos: Main – Walled path near Penmachno (Walk 10). *Inset* – Ysbyty Ifan. David Berry.

Care has been taken to be accurate. However neither the author nor the publisher can accept responsibility for any errors which may appear, or their consequences. If you are in any doubt about access, check before you proceed.

Printed by MWL, Pontypool.

ISBN: **978 1 902302 97 3**